1975

T5-AGJ-202

may be kept

FOURTEEN DAYS

time.

COMMUNITY

AND COMMUNICATIONS

By the same author
Boss Tweed's New York

COMMUNITY
AND
COMMUNICATIONS

Seymour J. Mandelbaum

W · W · NORTON & COMPANY · INC ·

New York

COPYRIGHT © 1972 BY W. W. NORTON & COMPANY, INC.

First Edition

Library of Congress Cataloging in Publication Data

Mandelbaum, Seymour J
 Community and communications.

 Includes bibliographical references.
 1. Communication—Social aspects—United States.
I. Title.
HM258.M17   301.14'0973   74-152670
ISBN 0-393-01001-5

PRINTED IN THE UNITED STATES OF AMERICA

1 2 3 4 5 6 7 8 9 0

For *Dorothy*, with love

CONTENTS

ACKNOWLEDGMENTS

This book was begun with the help of a Guggenheim Fellowship in the gracious setting of the Center for Advanced Study in the Behavioral Sciences. It was largely completed during a year in which I was released from teaching under a combined grant from the National Endowment for the Humanities and the Center for Urban Research and Experiment at the University of Pennsylvania. I am especially grateful to Professor Robert Mitchell, Director of the Center, for his encouragement.

Between the beginning and the end, I also received financial assistance from the Richard King Mellon and the John and Jane Martin Foundations, the Institute for Environmental Studies of the University of Pennsylvania, and the Annenberg School of Communications, also of the University of Pennsylvania. I hope this book in some measure repays the gift of time and trust.

Over the last several years of thinking and writing, I've been able to try out a great many ideas on students and colleagues and to learn from the interaction. I remember with particular fondness a joint seminar I taught together with Professor Rolf Meyersohn, now of the City University of New York, in 1967. Two students in the seminar, Ralph Hirsch of Drexel and Konrad K. Kalba of Harvard University, are now colleagues in the attempt to extend the range of communications planning. I've also enjoyed conversations with Pierre Calame, Benjamin Metalon, and Georges Mercadal of the Centre D'Études et de Recherches Sur L'Aménagement Urbain in Paris. The French group has published its reflections on communication patterns in a pamphlet, "Contribution à une Psycho-Sociologie Des Comportements Urbains: Structures urbaines, communication et comportement des menages."

9

Acknowledgments

On and off, from 1967 through 1969, I dreamed about actually initiating construction of a communications system in North Central Philadelphia. Though the dreams were not realized, the process was not, I think, for nought. I was helped in the process by Stanton Eckstut, who imagined what an open television studio and information center would look like, by Arthur Hall, who led a group of engineering graduate students in a hardware design, and by William Meek, then of the Area Wide Council of the Model Cities Program.

From 1966 to 1970, I was a member of the Ad Hoc Program Advisory Committee of the Center for Urban Education. I hope the chapters on education reflect some of the wisdom I absorbed from Robert Dentler, Director of the Center, and my colleagues on the committee. My reflections on the problems, possibilities, and limits of the traditional forms of community organization have been deepened by experiences in Camden, New Jersey, and the Wynnfield area of Philadelphia. I'm grateful to the many people who endured my theory in the midst of practical discussions. I'm also grateful to Starling Lawrence, an editor who helped me communicate.

This book, though short, has taken me longer to complete than I hoped. My major regret at the delay is that my father, Rabbi Albert N. Mandelbaum, did not live to see its completion.

This book is dedicated to Dorothy Rosenthal Mandelbaum, without whose love it never could have been completed. If the book helps to expand understanding, that will be my major legacy to our children, David, Judah, and Betsy.

Philadelphia
February, 1972

10

COMMUNITY
AND COMMUNICATIONS

ONE

PUBLIC UNDERSTANDING

This book is about the possibility that new communications systems will enhance public understanding. It describes a language, an historical perspective, and a set of ideas which may encourage this possibility. It does not describe, except in very general terms, the design of actual systems. Design is a detailed and sweaty task, hammered at over drawing boards and conference tables. The final chapter of this book, therefore, ends where conversations over those tables must begin.

The gravest danger in writing about communications is the banal repetition of what everyone knows. "We've got a communications problem," is probably the most fashionable item of popular social analysis. "Communicate!" is the eleventh commandment, or, in certain mouths, a revisionist addendum to the fifth.

The popular analysis and theology are not essentially wrong but they can be a suffocating blanket of good intentions. All conflict is robbed of meaning by the standard explanatory formula, *communications failure*, mechanically stamped on every episode. Admonitions to communicate with love and respect are soon corrupted by cynicism if the new spirit is not supported by new processes and rewards.

Throughout the pages which follow I have tried to follow three rules as hedges against banality and suffocation. I recommend them to the reader.

> *Assume, until shown otherwise, that conflicting groups and individuals understand each other perfectly.*
>
> *Assume, until shown otherwise, that men who do not consent to a socially wise course of action understand their own self-interest perfectly.*
>
> *Assume, until shown otherwise, that all calls to a new spirit of understanding and communication are cheap rhetorical tricks.*

Public understanding evokes for me two sets of connected questions:

> How can people come to know one another better, particularly across the barriers of class, race, ethnicity, nationality, and sex? How can they, even in conflict, transfer themselves imaginatively into their opponents' shoes? How can they use this ability of imaginative transference to find both satisfactory compromises and enlarged solutions in which conflicting goals become complementary?
>
> How can the governors of society come to understand better the nature of the system they lead, improve their ability to predict the outcomes of alternative policies, and successfully execute the preferred alternatives? How can large publics participate in choosing these alternatives?

The connection between these questions may not be immediately obvious because they appear to fall within two distinct domains of expertise. The specialists in human relations have explored the first set of questions. The library shelves are well-stocked with their volumes on intergroup prejudice and stereotypic thinking. The specialists in human relations have not, however, addressed the second set of questions, nor developed a persuasive model of change in which understanding matters. The man who is less prejudiced, we are led vaguely to expect, will express his openness in the myriad of his daily activities. These activities will somehow add up to a change in the tone and opportunities of our collective lives.

The governors and expert planners of society, who address themselves principally to the second set of questions, are understandably skeptical. Their job is to build cities and subdivisions; to maintain educational and transportation systems; to house men and to care for their health; to ensure their safety and their conformity to law. Their work begins with the analysis of the complex structural relationships between major components of the social system. Openness and a lack of prejudice may well be a necessary condition for change and creativity. They are, however, hardly sufficient. A man may be an enthusiastic advocate of racial integration and still approve of the market and educational processes which encourage segregation and educational failure. Goodness, unallied with knowledge, often frustrates itself.

Planners learn this frustration early in their professional lives and find reason and support for it in the literature of their professions. In 1798, Thomas Malthus warned against the dangers of imagining that charity would remedy the condition of the poor. Jay W. Forrester, expressing this old stricture in a new language, describes complex systems as "counterintuitive." Our everyday experience teaches us that if our hands are too cold, we warm them; if we want to drive our car, we turn the ignition. We wrongly generalize this experience with simple systems to complex ones and imagine—falsely, he asserts— that the way to improve the housing of the poor is to build low-cost housing. "Very often," Forrester cautions, "one finds that the policies that have been adopted for correcting a difficulty are actually intensifying it rather than producing a solution." [1]

Forrester undoubtedly exaggerates the complexity of the world to emphasize the newness of his own descriptions. His emphasis on counterintuitive systems, nevertheless, touches the tragic inadequacy of virtue without knowledge. As long as a good heart brought into the social arena leads to its own frustration, it is difficult to convince the doubters that life-seeking warmth and openness are better than the tussle of competitive selfishness. The spread of the values which

Charles Reich associates with Consciousness III in *The Greening of America* depends upon the engineering skills of Consciousness II.[2] Reich's book seems to me a rhetorical trick precisely because it obscures this dependence.

Planning professionals will certainly be flattered by an argument that their special knowledge is requisite for the development of heart or soul. (Soul, particularly, is a good thing to have these days and professionals are under heavy fire from those who claim it as a unique credential.) The professionals are not likely, however, to be pleased with the close linkage of what are often treated as opposing values. In public it is difficult to quarrel with a simultaneous call for more participation and more governance, more expert management and more intergroup understanding. Behind the scenes, where men wrestle with priorities, organizations, and analysis, reality makes short work of pious hopes and democratic symbols.

At one time or another, everyone, I suspect, has been charged with being unrealistic. When we counter this attack with a defense of our realism, we implicitly acknowledge how much reality is shaped by the eyes of the beholder. Observations and expectations, strategies attempted and strategies shunned, hopes and fears—all influence the way we define the amalgam of wisdom and practicality we call realism.

For most professional planners, this amalgam begins with a conviction that the world is growing constantly more interdependent and complex—the two ideas are hardly distinguished—and more rapidly changeful.[3] Vast networks of rapid transportation and virtually instantaneous communication extend the range of local acts so that their effects reverberate across the planet. Distant linguistic disputes, civil wars, sterilization campaigns, and student rebellions intrude into the most isolated of small towns and demand decisions in return. Time, measured by the discontinuity between one transaction and that which follows, is fragmented into smaller discrete moments. Change, measured by these finer units, is necessarily more rapid.

The global transformation of social scales takes different forms. At some moments in space and time, the movement has favored the creation of large out of what were once small, loosely connected units.

16

At other moments, large worlds—empires and giant business firms—have been divided and the parts connected in new ways. With each shift in interdependence and complexity, however, power has shifted to the men who uniquely trade in cosmopolitan knowledge. In the United States, this shift has, for the most part, associated professional expertise with the movement towards larger units of business and government, and from legislative to executive political dominance. Even suburban planners, however, who earn their wages defending against this movement, depend upon their knowledge of the whole urban system in order to protect their clients against the encroachments of the city.

The need for his expertise is the second item in the professional definition of realism. Respect for expertise is, of course, never adequate in the planners' mind, but it must certainly grow in time. Failure to match the expansion of complexity with expertise will lead—in the most pessimistic view—to a social and environmental apocalypse.

Practicing planners and politicians are likely to speak softly about the realistic need for their services and their expanding power. Theorists of the distant future are less constrained. Whether apprehensively or hopefully, most of the members of the flourishing club of futurists expect a major realignment of political power in favor of the experts.[4] Reform will be even further professionalized. New or whispered quantitative forecasting and planning techniques, symbolized but not really described by images of giant computers, will broaden the gap between the wide-ranging vision of those who know and the narrow, selfish perspective of the uninformed and incompetent. Representative institutions, already in world-wide decline, will lose still further initiative. In the futurist projection, the tasks of creating public agreement will fall increasingly to executive agencies designed to plan and administer public policies. To accomplish this task, they will develop new norms for consultation and public hearings. It is not likely, however, that these norms (amounting to a new constitution for democratic government) will yield as much substance as show. The interconnection of agencies stretching across conventional political boundaries will isolate them from any spatially bounded constituency which can hold them accountable. Already, a description of the government of a major American city which ended at the city line would be incredibly naive; a campaign for mayor in which candidates pretended that they could control the "city government" would be a fog of deception.

Experts on the front lines of governmental agencies may take some hidden delight at the futurist projection. For the moment, however, faced with the reality of mass participation in their domains, they are often reduced to a hidden grumble. If only the voters weren't so narrow minded. . . ," the grumble begins. "If only everyone didn't want to stick his two-cents and his clumsy thumb into the pie. . . . If only urbanity and civility could be revived . . . ," it concludes. I suspect that even the most ardent democrats have expressed these feelings at one time or another. I doubt that any practicing professional has been immune from the suspicion that, realistically, the will of the people has been the most potent enemy of the public good.[5]

Reality is impressive, but not impenetrable.

It is difficult to argue on formal grounds with the belief in the increase of complexity. By almost every measure, social roles are more highly differentiated today than they were in 1800 or in 1900. There is every reason to think that roles will be more specialized still in the year 2000. Integrating these roles demands an expansion of public communication processes and functions. A jack-of-all-trades may talk to himself as he moves from act to act but his thoughts leave no trace. A chain of surgeon-internist-resident-nursing supervisor-floor nurse-orderly-nutritionist-paraprofessional trails a wake of charts and orders behind. All the interactions in that chain, all the messages, all the chances for messing up, selectively improving, or adapting to threat and opportunity define the structure of complexity.

The expansion of complexity does not, however, necessarily imply an increased rapidity of change. If separate interpersonal transactions are multiplied in any unit of time, then the future is more changeful. The pattern of transactions may, however, be remarkably stable over time. There is really no special reason to believe that the change in life styles between 1970 and the year 2000 is either harder to predict or likely to be more dramatic than the leap between 1940 and 1970, 1910 and 1940, 1870 and 1910.[6] Indeed, for the overwhelming percentage of Americans the great transformations seem to lie in the past: the move from one culture to another, the migration from farm to city, the electronic expansion of perceptual fields.

The great shock of the future, as it creeps up upon us in simple tomorrows, is likely to be how much it manages to resemble yesterday.

Increased complexity does not even necessarily imply increased interdependence within parts of an already established system. In the United States, the major changes shaping a web of national interdependence are already behind us: the commercialization of agriculture and the virtual elimination of rural home manufacturing and urban farming. The rate of interstate migration has hardly changed over the last century. The continental diffusion of knowledge of urban consumption patterns is virtually complete. Indeed, the spread of opportunities has, on many dimensions, attenuated the lines of connection between spaces and groups. New York is less the national metropolis than it was in 1900. Suburbs have gained an industrial base which reduces their dependence on central cities.[7]

The widespread perception that cities are unsafe or may destroy themselves cannot, it seems to me, be explained by the growth of interdependence. The source lies elsewhere. For at least a century, middle- and upper-class urbanites have successfully protected their values by spatially segregating themselves from the poor and militarily controlling the dangerous classes. These protective strategies have not been merely defensive illusions. They have, as their most positive ideologists have contended, shaped a new city providing ease of movement, healthy environments, spacious housing, and recreational facilities to a broad range of the population.

These protective and creative strategies have been pursued with particular vigor since World War II. Precisely, however, as an idea is explicitly articulated and dominates public policy, its limits become sharply apparent. The popular perception of crisis reflects a loss of confidence in the adequacy of traditional strategies of segregation and control, a suspicion that the creation of the new city did not quite solve all of the problems of the old. This loss of confidence and this suspicion are thoroughly reasonable. They cannot, however, be used to validate the professional ideology of reality.

Most of what is professionally described as the reality of interdependence, complexity, and rapid change I see as chiefly a comment on the expansion of knowledge. Professionals are particularly prone to believe that the world is knowable and that society can collectively shape its future. A gap in knowledge, a lapse in control, or an ambitious plan for a yet unrealized future is perceived as a growth in complexity.

In a similar manner, professional planners are bound to grumble about the limits of participation and democracy. The professionals, in a wide variety of institutions, characteristically describe their principal interest as the "public good." This concept (sometimes under other names) is very old, widely employed, and in some disrepute. The disrepute and associated suspicions are not undeserved. Actions to enhance the public good always manage to cost some groups more than others. Wrapped in the mantle of the general interest, men try to outvote the actual parents of today's children by appeal to the silent and infinitely expandable generations to come.

The idea of the public good is not, however, without its honest purposes. In a particular situation of conflict between two or more parties, the public good may be defined as the solution in which parties find that they can satisfy all or most of their important goals without sacrificing groups outside themselves. Planning professionals —in social work, in education, in land use, in transportation, in housing, or income support—tend to hold, as a basic article of belief, that there are arrays of solutions in each of their fields which would satisfy apparently conflicting parties. In a dispute between advocates of more vocational or more academic education, the planner finds a curriculum which generates both greater theoretical richness and more effective job training. In a dispute between proponents of higher income support levels and of reduced taxes, the planner believes there is a way to make us all wealthier and all more secure.

The belief in the possibility of these solutions and the concern with finding them distinguishes planners, as ideal types, from politicians. (Real men, of course, play both roles and sometimes wear the wrong job label). Politicians largely focus on finding compromise solutions which allow conflicting parties enough satisfaction so that they do not attack the governing structure or personnel. The planner's image of mutually satisfying, higher-order solutions, explains why, at first blush, popular attitudes seem so hostile to the public good. The advocates of a particular position in a conflict, by their very partisanship, make it difficult to find the higher solutions which relocate and reorganize the domain of possibilities in which the battle has been set. Racists, on both sides of the color line, impede the creation of a mutually satisfying integrated society. Proponents of high standards as an instrument of action limit the chances of improving the productivity of the educational system.

People cannot be faulted for resisting attempts to reconceptualize issues about which they care a great deal. Every proposed new solution is a prediction about the impact of future behavior. Such predictions are the most important instrument with which individuals organize and manage their environments. There is every reason to be cautious in replacing tested with untried strategies.[8]

Where conflict exists, the more people who are mobilized, the harder it is to invent a shared idea of the public good. Novices in the planning professions may laud participation, but experienced hands know better. Mobilization is for winning a political battle, or for enlisting cooperation, not for imaginative planning. Understandably, futurists who are confident that new tools of analysis or forecasting will suggest creative but imaginatively remote solutions anticipate a shift in political power, reducing or at least redirecting participation.

The planner's complaint with participation is intrinsic to his role and, therefore, presents an intractable communications problem. No amount of broadly shared knowledge or imaginative capacity will reduce the necessary limitations of advocacy in the midst of conflict. The complaint should not, however, be endowed with excessive significance. In any particular situation, parties to a dispute may be perfectly capable of abandoning old conceptions for new and grasping innovative solutions. The extent of this capability depends upon many factors, including the processes available to them for examining their own assumptions critically and trying new ideas or behaviors tentatively and experimentally. Often this means being able to watch other people, learning from them vicariously and with little personal risk.

Proposals to reduce participation cannot be used as substitutes for

21

learning. Lecturing people about civility cannot reduce the need for understanding. There is no practically feasible nor ethically appropriate way to expand the domain of expertise in the United States except by increasing the intellectual capabilities of large publics so that they may deal complexly with reality. Forecasts of a future shift in which knowledge triumphs over ignorance ignore this requirement only by treating present difficulties as anachronistic, conjuring up a never-never land in which they will disappear: whites will consent to school integration, suburbanites will change their land use preferences, communities will treat clean water and air as scarce resources, taxpayers will not revolt in waves of irrational resentment.

This book is about the expansion of public understanding. It moves back and forth between the intellectual concerns of the human relations experts and those of planners, hopefully uniting them in a new way. It begins with an analysis of human communication and moves from there to new possibilities in the sharing of experiences, the development of learning processes, and the interpenetration of professional and public roles. Its general method is to move from history to policy, describing through the first the appropriate beginning points and boundaries of the second.

T W O

COMMUNITY AND COMMUNICATIONS

When I first began to think about this book, the image in my head was that a city is a communications network.[1] Building on that image, it was appropriate to ask, How does the network operate? and, subsequently, How may its performance be improved?

It has taken me a long time to learn that my initial image, because it accepts the ordinary language of urban description at its beginning, was leading me into conceptual and political dead ends. My difficulties deserve some explication because the ordinary language is deeply embedded in scholarly as well as popular usage. I'm not alone, I'm sure, in trying to add a new idea to an old structure without fully realizing how much change the innovation requires.

The ordinary language of urban description builds upon an image of the city as a bounded territory, marked off from both adjacent rural and the next urban spaces. The boundary is defined in the practice of the Census Bureau by a series of measures: a drop in density, an increase in agricultural labor, and a reduction in commuting, telephoning, shopping, and shared newspaper reading between the city and its out-area. This city is, in turn, subdivided into a series of smaller territories. The most important dividing lines delimit a vast array of political units. Some of these appear on a map as city, borough, and township boundaries. Others, just as real but less obvious and more changeable, mark off special sewer, water, police, school, and planning districts.

The importance of spatial political boundaries reflects the resolution of a debate on the logic of representative institutions which has engaged western nations for several centuries. There have been broadly two positions in this debate. Proponents of the first have argued that members of society should be classified and represented through their participation in interest groups, estates, guilds, or classes. Proponents of the second position have insisted that classification and representation should depend on residence within spatial units.

This second position has wholly carried the day in the structuring of formal representative institutions. Even if no other influence had intervened, spatial boundaries had the enormous benefit of being analytically and politically feasible. Individuals play so many social roles in the same gross moment in space and time that it would be impossible to represent them rationally according to their interests. Residence appeared to obey the simple laws of physics: a person could only live in one space at any one time. (Multiple home ownership and rapid mobility complicate this judgment and yield very grave political difficulties).

The proponents of interest representation were not entirely defeated. Their view is expressed in the vast political world of private associations, organized pressure groups, and even specialized regulatory agencies. Though enormously powerful, this is in some ways a demi-world of suspicions and questions. Compare, for illustration of this lowly status, the legitimacy attached to the tokens of membership. We talk, on the one hand, of special interests; on the other, of the citizen.

When these two systems of representation overlap, the tension between them generates ideological and overt political stress. Reformers have repeatedly fastened on the "senator from the steel industry," or the "railroad congressman," as objects of attack. It seems clearly illegitimate, though very lucrative, for the representative of a spatial area to select a small group among his constituents and to become their representative. The balance of legitimacy tips the other way, however, when segregation transforms interest politics into spatial politics. What the prosperous cannot claim as a class, a rich suburb can demand as a community.

The spatial organization of representative institutions has extensive influence over our social and political imagery. The U.S. Census is one of the principal instruments of this influence. For at least a century, the census takers have gone beyond their simple constitutional mandate. They now provide the largest uniform body of social data available to private and public planners. Almost all of this data, however, is filtered through the template of spatial units. Despite the best efforts of the counters to sophisticate their measures, the bias of space remains: small and scattered groups are easy to lose, the experience of classes and roles through time is difficult to follow.[2]

From the perspective of the politician and policy maker, spatial categories and spatial change always have had a seductive appeal. A new facility is a great deal more tangible than "increased opportunity." An attack on crime directed to "cleaning up the neighborhood" is more visible than a change in the penal system which reduces the flow of repeat offenders. The very language of politics is pervaded with spatial images. In the old style, it was common to see the city as an aggregate of neighborhoods. In the new style of political discourse, the same perceptions reappear. Decentralization is assumed to be a strategy for the relocation of authority within small spatial units. "Community control of the schools," means control by the surrounding inhabitants. "The university should help its community," is a call for assistance to immediate neighbors. The census organization of detailed knowledge around spatial categories simply reinforces the bias to do what can be seen and readily described. Even if no other influences intervened, it would be difficult to avoid slipping from a description of the poor to a picture of places called ghettos or slums. It would be hard to avoid moving from an attack on poverty to a program of community or neighborhood renewal.

The major difficulties of the spatial image can be illustrated by a fictional, but not unreal, example.[3] A man may live in Oshkosh where the factory in which he works requires its employees to be physically present five days a week for most of the year. This requirement is quite general in the world of work but it is by no means universal. There are jobs which call for sustained absence from the base site, as in the case of traveling salesmen. In the future, our man in Oshkosh—or his job—may change to allow more prolonged absence or greater distance between the actual site of work and the firm's base of operations.

Our man's income and the cost and time of travel under existing conditions encourage him to live within a few minutes car ride from the plant. Changes in these conditions may radically alter this preference in the future. Even in the here and now, however, his place of residence does not totally circumscribe his realm of interactions. Every week he may talk deeply and personally on the telephone with old friends or family in other cities. With his neighbors, an occasional pleasantry may suffice. His entertainment may come from New York and Hollywood, his children go to college in Madison, his political attention be riveted on Washington.

Describing Oshkosh as this man's community, that is, as his essential network of interactions or communication, is clearly false. To ask that he join his community by talking with his neighbors on the other side of the tracks is dishonest and, under many circumstances, useless. It is, of course, perfectly legitimate to ask him to change his community by dealing with new people or in new ways. This request can never have the moral imperative assumed in the spatial model. It must, therefore, always include some calculus of cost and benefit which is credible to the man from Oshkosh—and to all of the millions like him whom we would like to reach. "Why," we must allow him to ask, "should I talk with those people?"

The same calculus is, of course, required for the most intensely local urbanite. While there is virtually no one in an American city who is free of the networks of the cosmopolitan from Oshkosh, we have become newly sensitive in recent years to the persistence of urban patterns in which some men live, work, marry, shop, and visit within closely bounded neighborhoods. We can no more ask these "villagers"[4] to extend their communicative range to the city as a whole as a matter of natural right than we can demand that the cosmopolitan from Oshkosh redirect or narrow his.

The first step in developing a morally credible basis for this calculus, is to abandon the spatial model of the city and the association of the word *community* with a pattern of settlement.

A man's community is, quite simply, the set of people, roles, and places with whom he communicates.

Every simple definition hides, of course, its own special set of difficulties. The first difficulty here is the separation of communication from all the myriad forms of human interchange. Men are linked together in extended networks through which they exchange goods, services, and energy. No stretch of nomenclature will turn all the items flowing through these networks into bits of information. An orange shipped from Florida to New York remains an orange and cannot be magically transformed into a unit of knowledge.

There is associated with the orange, however, and with every other item exchanged between men, some symbolic information. This information plays a vital role in the preservation and evolution of the system of interaction. Without the information, behavior would consist of isolated acts, without possibilities of either continuity or learning. With it, items such as an orange signal a delighted buyer that similar purchases will convey pleasure on repeated occasions. The money he puts down on the counter similarly tells the grower that profits are to be made in New York and that it's worthwhile sending another shipment northward.

The information attached to the orange is not an isolated bit with an intrinsic quality of its own. Most purchasers in the United States treat the individual orange as a member of a class of goods of essentially similar character which can be obtained through the repetition of the same buying behavior in the future. In another time and place, a purchaser might regard the orange as a unique entity which he could never hope to reproduce by any conceivable act of his own. The orange does not so much carry as evoke or select a meaning. Its symbolic attributes are in the mind of the beholder, and beyond his mind, in the whole array of ideas and processes of learning in which he has been involved. It is these ideas and processes which give sustained meaning to the orange and to all other exchanges. A flow of goods, in one system of thought, may signify freedom from drudgery, a release of creative opportunities, and a fulfillment of cherished dreams. In another system, they are marked with the labels of crass materialism, enslaving men and limiting their horizons. The goods are the same in either case.

An analytical and political focus on the exchange of symbolic meaning turns attention to these ideas and communication processes. The danger in this focus is that the oranges are easily forgotten. Human beings are amazing animals who can delight in the play of symbols and create vast institutions whose only ostensible purpose is to facilitate symbolic interchange. Under most conditions, however, communication serves some external end, whether it be the consumption of oranges, the amelioration of disease, or the production of automobiles. Within these systems of action, meaning and purpose are inextricably linked. Communications policy must tread a narrow path between the equally deceptive assumptions that meaning will inevitably come trailing after action or that action will be totally responsive to a transformation of understanding.

When systems for developing and sharing symbolic meaning are working well, we hardly notice them. They merge into the institutions and patterns of action which they support. When events go badly, however, we become self-conscious about the meanings attached to exchanges: a politician blunders, we send the wrong grain to relieve a famine, fathers and sons drift apart for lack of understanding.

In each of these troubled cases, the object of our attention is some particular missed meaning, some gap in communications. There are two complementary approaches to these difficulties. The first is to close the gap by correcting misperceptions and supplying missing understanding. Both in the most creative segments of the political sphere and in the scholarly world, earnest men and women apply themselves to the task of listening to one group and conveying its intentions to another.

The second approach, to which this book is largely devoted, concentrates on the design of the networks of communication rather than the conveyance of particular messages. A great many things, it seems to me, cannot be said through the available networks. Better books will not alter the intrinsic limitations of the present library system; better television programs will not remedy the faults of a massive system which is unresponsive to the queries of an individual viewer.

The very act of creating new messages frequently depends upon the reshaping of communication patterns, rather than simply heightened attention or sympathy. White construction workers—picking a case which illustrates this dependence—are often accused of prejudice or, more sympathetically, of not understanding blacks. I suspect that the reverse is true: they understand them all too well. The whites feel threatened precisely because they comprehend the nature of black demands and the claims of black humanity. More jobs for under-privileged blacks mean fewer jobs for working-class whites. What they do not understand are the messages about industrial futures which might satisfy all of the parties in conflict. "Understanding" these messages is, of course, a euphemism. The messages have first to be created in a rich interaction between planners and contestants. which goes beyond confrontation, mediation, coercion, or even human relations counseling.

There are immediate costs to the decision to focus on the design of systems of communication rather than the conveyance of missed meanings. The language of meaning and of creative understanding is rich with personal affect: rage and friendship, suspicion and hope. The language of systems is more impersonal, indeed even seems to be directed towards mechanizing man.

There is no simple way to mitigate this charge and the suspicion it engenders. The language needed to shape an image and measure the dimensions of human communication is, in fact, designed to facilitate the mechanization of intelligent functions and the expansion of remote electronic communication. Whether you label telephones, computers, satellites, and cable television systems as inhuman and mechanizing or as liberating should, however, depend on their effects and not on their peculiar technology.

All communication processes require some connecting technology.

When we bring several people together in a living room to talk with one another we hardly think about the room and the streets they walked to get there as technological components. When the same people are connected in a television conference, the machines are harder to ignore. In part, our heightened perception of the technology may be simply a matter of custom and expectation. It is possible, for example, to become so used to telephone conversation that one forgets the machine. Beyond the desensitization which comes with use, however, lies a real and ineluctable difference between direct and remote encounters. The image of a man transmitted through an electrical impulse can never be the same as the image seen directly. The development of new technologies of communication offers more partial—because mechanized—contacts than ever before in human history. The issue for personal choice would be simple if all of these contacts could be supported wholly and richly without the inter-mediaries of books or television, telephones or computers. The choice is, unfortunately, not so simple. Each of the losses with mechanization is the price paid for some benefit.

Again, the balance of costs and benefits, rather than the fact of mechanization, should be the measure of value.

The spatial image of the city describes the pattern of community life in the localization of populations and roles: factories here, houses there; expensive homes here, slums there. The communications model begins with three components of every network:

- an *intelligence center,* which performs several functions, each located in a specialized subcenter: it scans the environment, receives and transmits messages, encoding and decoding them as it goes, processes information, and stores it.

- a *channel* for the conveyance of messages.

- a *code* onto which meaning can be impressed and from which it can be deciphered.

In any real communications system, the boundaries set around each of these components depends upon the scale at which the system is observed. A human being, for example, may be treated as an intelligence center sending messages out through external channels, or he may be looked at as a complete network, with internal channels and codes. Similarly, a television station is both channel and complete system. Even the English language, usually conceived as simply a code, may be treated as a full network, replete with norm-setters (hipsters and research scientists) and legitimating institutions (dictionaries and news commentators).

Each of the components may be described as having an observed level of use. A man, for example, may be speaking slowly, a library may contain a million books, or a city may have two television channels. For the planner trying to build a different future, the present level of use is, however, only a partial guide to the possibilities of each component. He needs a measure of the capacities of channels, codes, and processors. How quickly—or slowly—may a man speak and still be understood? How many books can the library hold? How many T.V. stations may be fitted into the frequency band?

Capacity is measured on three dimensions:

the volume of information which can be handled in a unit of time.

the syntactical complexity of the information which can be handled.

the range of the component

The capacity and range of some components are intrinsic in their physical nature and are unchangeable. Mathematical communications theory, as developed by Claude Shannon and others, is a set of statements about the absolute capacity of idealized channels to convey information.[5] The measure of a unit of information in this formal theory is a *bit,* described as the amount of information necessary to indicate which of two alternatives is indicated in a signal. In the classic example, it takes one bit to tell whether a flipped coin has landed on heads or tails. The capacity of a channel is measured by the number of bits it can convey in a unit of time. Since the channels used for electronic communication and perhaps even the neural chains in man approximate the idealized conditions, the formal theory describes intractable constants in the design of physical networks.

Other measures of volume and most of range are not based in absolute physical limits but in relatively stable but still changeable social conditions. The scope of attention,' how many people have television sets, the location of libraries and book sellers, the cost of telephones and magazines, the boundaries of a linguistic community —all of these dimensions of range are socially derived. Even the physical limits of the range of a television or radio signal can be extended by a social decision to relay the message.

The capacity to handle syntactical complexity also seems in most systems to be a social rather than a physical variable. Aside from the simplest forms of experimental situations, the theoretical limits of human processing capacities are hardly ever broached. Human beings manage to organize knowledge into syntactically rich, general concepts from which particulars can be derived. This allows them to bring what would be impossible tasks within their capacities.[6]

Individuals vary in their ability to perform these organizational tasks. These variations may, indeed, be largely what we measure in intelligence tests. Quite apart from genetic endowments, however, the individual variations seem to be conditioned by the linguistic codes men have learned to speak, write, and read.[7] The first difference between codes is in vocabulary: in one, everyone may be "sick in the head"; in another, schizophrenia and paranoia each has a different verbal flag. The second syntactical difference is in the array of connective devices linking ideas to one another. The most obvious example of syntactic richness is the series of *whereases* and *whomsoevers* in legal documents, boggling the mind of all but the trained lawyers. Less obvious, are the patternings in paragraphs such as this one, which make complex prose difficult for a great many readers who understand easily each of the separate words.

The verbal code, even at its best, has severe limits. To imagine, let alone convey, a pattern of interaction between twenty variables, I would switch from words to mathematical symbols and statements —if I had learned the language of mathematics more thoroughly. Having failed to learn properly, there are some ideas I can hardly comprehend or communicate.

The estimated capacities of individual components do not add up mechanically to the attributes of the entire communications network.

There are qualities of the system as a whole which describe its development through time. I call these qualities, internal and external integration.

External integration is simply the linkage of the communications system proper with the system of action. This linkage may be rapid, as in a network for the automatic control of traffic flows, or it may be delayed, as in schools which send their graduates into the work force after years of preparation. The linkage may be concentrated in one stage of the system, as in publishing where only the final product matters, or may be scattered through the components. In every case, however, the existing or necessary links between communications and action is a central concern of a networks designer. The literature on public information, for example, reports the percentages of Americans who do not know the name of the Chief Justice or the members of the Cabinet, or who do not understand the dynamics of this or that public program.[8] The usual response to these percentages, after the initial sighs of disappointment and allusions to democratic theory are concluded, is to urge more civic education through the schools and mass media. Frequently, however, the major limitations on public knowledge reside in the direct system of action itself. The political system does not tell people that the specified knowledge would be rewarded. It is the lack of rewards, rather than the limits of the communications network, which constricts public knowledge. The schools may teach and the media proclaim but the intended message still does not get through. The message which may get through, is, moreover, likely to be very different from conventional civic wisdom. People learn that the world is either incomprehensible or deceptive.

The internal integration of a communications network measures the relationship between the components of a system. Each of the components, particularly when they are institutionalized in forms such as newspapers, television stations, and libraries, take on an independent life of their own, partially free of the pressure of the other elements. The shape of the actual network operating for an individual or group, however, depends upon the link between components. A man may be exposed to a great many messages, but lacking facilities for remembering them, he quickly focuses on a narrow part of the whole. If I were to be cut off from a library, I would devote a great deal more of my attention to the tedious learning of detailed information. Like a local sage, I would become a storehouse of knowledge and wisdom about a little world drawn around me.

It would be conveniently simple to imagine that communications networks are limited by their weakest components: over time, men will not pay attention to information which they can neither process nor store; they will not try to remember what they cannot manage to hear.

The modes of adjusting to limitations are, however, richer than the simple image suggests. There are two major modes. The first is to devote more time to a function. Most people have probably had the experience of straining to listen to and understand a complex statement meant properly to be read. Direct speech can lend personal emphasis and authority to ideas but it is very difficult to process complex information which is received solely by listening. The limits of the channel can be ameliorated, however, if the message is repeated. "Say that again," we ask the speaker.

The second mode of adjustment is to replace one function with another. If I have a weak long-term memory, I can establish transmission lines in compensation. "I don't have a pencil," I've sometimes been forced to tell a caller. "Telephone later to remind me."

The image of components and networks—with levels of usage and measures of capacity and integration attached to each—is the framework of analysis throughout the rest of this book. Each of the chapters uses the image to define a perspective on a particular policy issue. Three observations, however, define a general outlook which pervades all of the chapters.

1. *Over the last century, the cost of the transmission of information over long distances has been reduced proportionally more than over short. The same relative cost relationship is likely to continue in the future.*[9]

The major source of this cost relationship is the technology of the electronic media. Major fixed costs in these media—notably terminals and switching centers—are not notably increased with the extension of distance. Indeed, some technologies are such that more is less, farther is cheaper. Similar relationships appear also in transportation systems. The absolute cost differences—measured in both time and real dollars—between intra- and intercity travel has been dramatically reduced over the century. (This reduction is particularly striking for remote cities; less notable in the eastern megalopolis.)

This cost relationship has reshaped the national and international flow of messages. In 1870, in any American city, the volume of messages processed sloped downward with the distance of the city from the source of the message. Local speech, local newspapers, local sermons, schools, and plays had large audiences; occasional touring companies and remotely published magazines and books commanded smaller numbers. Over the last century, distant messages—television shows, mass magazines, movies, records and radio—have radically shifted and twisted portions of the curve. Nothing may have quite replaced local talk, but young children do appear to spend more time with television than with their neighborhood school.

The shifting and twisting of the curve has been perceived as both an opportunity and a danger, as a source of freedom and as the death of intimate communities.[10] I am less interested in these contrasting perceptions, however, than in the seductions of the cost relationships for communications planning. The relative cheapness of remote communications should not necessarily imply that investments in remote transmission are more important than an expansion of local capacities. A communications network is more than a channel. Unless new means of remote transmission are complemented by local facilities for processing, then the flow of messages may obscure as much as clarify. India, via satellite, becomes simply one more television spectacular, emotionally remote though visually close. Even the most ardent cosmopolitan, once he is sensitive to the internal integration of the network, may reasonably decide that clarification calls for apparently expensive investments in local communication rather than the alluring pursuit of distance.

2. *The external and internal integration of communications networks are positively related.*

The point of this observation is that men are not likely to tolerate ineffective communication where its costs are clear and repeated.

Clumsy work directions which lead to production errors and losses are usually withdrawn and rewritten. Hospital administrators grow disenchanted with large data gathering projects when there doesn't seem to be any way of using the information gathered at great expense.

The discipline of rewards and punishments is less likely to work in networks whose purposes are vague, delayed, or suspect. In government, where the test of profitability rarely applies, large amounts of information are gathered but are neither analyzed, communicated, nor used. There are, in the same way, very few tests of the effectiveness of a university as a communications network. As a result, the parts of the network are often a crazy quilt of mismatched capacities.

This observation leads to a design principle: if you want internally to integrate a communications network through the expansion of particular component capacities—such as the ability of people to read or to understand—link the network to a clear purpose and reward.

This principle is also a warning of difficulties: Where a communications network is internally integrated around a clear external purpose, it is very hard to expand the network's capacity without major social displacement. The local communications network of an Indian village, a neighborhood in an American city, or a private organization, may be well adapted for one set of purposes. Increasing the capacity of the network may leave these purposes unattended, threaten established roles and norms, and generate anxiety and fear.

This warning would be easier to accept were people not so remarkably inventive in creating purposes for the symbols they find around them. Far from the usual assumptions of the general desire for escape, most men and women seem to me passionately to desire serious communication. They want symbols to have purpose and meaning. Many critical observers, for example, are aghast at the irrelevance and incomprehensibility of American television. The medium, for reasons intrinsic to its design, seems as little able to convey a complex idea as is a village parade. The differences between well and poorly educated groups in their understanding of world affairs remain today much the same as they were the 1930s before the explosion of home television.[11]

A proposal to change American television should not, however, begin with a glib assumption that parades are irrelevancies which can be ignored. They are serious and well-integrated communication modes. They are play activities, full of ritual meanings which are easily grasped because they are so fully shared and so little examined (hence the dominance of sports). Even the announcement of bad news may have a comforting quality. Everything must be under control if a trusted figure proclaims the disorder.

A parade is also a collective fantasy—not an escape from reality but a set of clues to the structure of society and norms of behavior beyond the boundaries of immediate acquaintance. The clues are there no matter how symbolic, playful, sleezy, or imaginary the program. The lower class teenagers reported in one study who described television as very real and true to life viewed it, I suspect, from this clue-taking perspective.[12] They were neither stupid nor deceived, nor can they be cheated of their parade without an adequate replacement.

3. *The components of the communications networks actually available to groups in the population differ in their usage and capacities. The broader these differences, the greater the likelihood that equalization in the usage or available capacities of any single component will require major changes in the total pattern of network relationships.*

The fact of these differences is obvious—though its dimensions are sometimes shocking. Certainly a quarter, and perhaps more than a half of United States adults could not manage to wade their way through this book, even if they tried.[13] An even larger number would probably be hard pressed to discover a way of buying or borrowing it, even if they knew it existed. Similarly, while virtually every American can conveniently view television programs, very few can produce them.

The connection between these differences and the general pattern of the communications network is less obvious and is often painfully ignored. Use and access to communications components—whether they be libraries, television sets, or English—is stratified where the differences endow some people with greater control over material resources. Speaking is more commanding than listening; writing, in many circumstances, more powerful still. Accordingly, virtually everyone in the United States is able to understand standard English speech; a substantially smaller number is able to speak it, an even smaller group able to write it coherently.

The idea of coherence is, of course, a group norm largely designed to preserve the stratification of capacities. Powerful writing behavior is often suppressed under the charge that it is incoherent. A similar suppression may occur when behavior embedded in a particular situation is treated as an intractable personal attribute. In the last several years sociolinguists have described important differences in the verbal codes of English speakers. Basil Bernstein, the best-known of the linguists, argues that some speakers usually from the working class, talk in a restricted code, useful for signalling assent or relating to authority but maladapted to the explication of both complex and new meanings. He contrasts this restricted code with the more extended pattern common in the middle class.[14]

Edward Banfield, the conservative political scientist, reads Bernstein's work, and those of his students and colleagues, as delineating an impassable obstacle to complex communication and planning in lower class populations.[15] Banfield ignores, however, the major point of the sociolinguistic enterprise. Verbal behavior in a stratified system is functionally related to the situations speakers see before them. With a believable change in situations, and the development of trust, restricted speakers elaborate their meaning. Indeed, Bernstein's initial distinction may be seriously biased by the experimental situation itself. A wise child, as William Labov notes in a critical review, may say as little as possible in an interview "where anything he says can literally be held against him." [16] The suspicion which underlies that wisdom may be based in class experiences, and may be embedded in linguistic practice, but it is not an impassable obstacle to communication.

Equalizing the linguistic repertoires of social classes depends upon an equalization of their need and ability to cope with varied environments. There is a chicken and egg dilemma to this dependence. Need is usually linked to ability; ability to linguistic competence. This dilemma is not unusual in social policy. It demands that changes be made in different parts of the social system or communications network, simultaneously or in proper phasing. Acting on the isolated component—even with the best of egalitarian intentions—ends usually in frustration. A new instructional method does not convince people to read unless literacy matters. Making literacy matter, where print is power, requires more than a new instructional method.

Having abandoned the spatial model of the city I can now turn back with a new image in mind to reexamine the influence of spatial arrangements upon communication and community building. The next chapter is particularly devoted to the question, How important is the reorganization of space to the expansion of intergroup understanding and the expansion of public competence?

THREE

THE REORGANIZATION
OF SPACE

The simplest observation to make about space and communication is that cities must be good for something. If a capricious god had randomly scattered people across the face of the earth, here and there clusters would be apparent. There would, however, not have been so many of them, nor would they have grown so prodigiously in the last century and a half, if propinquity were not an advantage for some human interactions.

Moving beyond that simple observation to detail the nature of the advantage and the interactions enters a tangle of scholarly dispute. The substance of this dispute is irrelevant to the problem of social understanding; its logic is central. Many analysts—both expert and lay—subtly transform the question, "What is the function of cities?" into the future-oriented-query, "What are the appropriate criteria for their design?" The search for criteria easily turns back into history, as if the appropriate purposes of urban areas could be deciphered from their origins. This is the hidden meaning behind the debate over the first cities in which Lewis Mumford so delights: Were they intended for trade, for protection, or for free and varied social interaction? [1]

The circuitous path from function to futures and back to history is not confined, of course, to the analysis of cities. Arguments about the future of both religion and the nation are frequently fought on the battlegrounds of the past. The appeal to origins and founders serves an important function in preserving the continuity of social institutions. It masks, however, a confusion of analysis and preference. Cities may be designed to satisfy a wide variety of criteria. At present, and whatever their past, their gross outlines are dominated by a single influence.

That influence is work. Men gather in cities in awesome numbers because propinquity is rewarded in the organization of work processes. The work may go on in business firms or government offices; in laboratories or on assembly lines. In any case, it is work and not variety, sociability, freedom, or protection which holds large cities together. Migrants may be recruited for many reasons but they remain and the clusters are sustained because of the advantages of working closely together. There are many cities in the present and in the past where the forces of recruitment and retention seem badly out of kilter. The disparities are often, however, more apparent than real. In Calcutta, where great masses of workless peasants crowd the streets, what stands revealed is not so much the false myth of the city as the poverty of the village.

Our knowledge of the actual relationship between the gross fact of concentrations of populations in small areas and the organization of work is relatively limited. We have in hand a series of observations about the related occurrence of particular industrial and particular urban developments. These observations, linked by a fragile body of economic theory, reduce the uncertainty attached to a series of decisions in which relatively little is at stake. A firm may be helped, for example, to choose a site in which workers may be recruited, its products efficiently produced, and then cheaply shipped to market. Comparably, a city or regional agency may encourage economic development in a promising industrial sector or geographic area. Our knowledge boggles, however, before larger and more risk-ridden problems. We could, if we willed, build a generation of wholly new cities designed to enhance values which are depressed in older sites. What would be the impact of such a choice on the total national economic performance? Would the individual cities be economically viable? If they were not, would they be worth subsidizing? Why? [2]

These questions are extremely difficult to answer. (Even the proper asking entails more precision than I have engaged.) This difficulty restricts public action and reinforces the grip of free market decision-making.

In the twentieth century, these market processes have been remarkably respectful of established urban forms. During the first part of the nineteenth century, industrial enterprises frequently developed and prospered in small village settings. Substantial settlements were almost wholly concentrated around water-transport routes, performing commercial services for an agrarian population. In the last half of the century, the manufacturing advantage changed and a great array of industrial cities entered the urban hierarchy. Established commercial centers were, for the most part, also able to capitalize on industrial development and retained their place as major cities. In a few cases, however, such old commercial settlements as New Orleans, Charleston, and Albany clearly lost ground to such new giants as Pittsburgh, Cleveland, Detroit, Milwaukee, and Buffalo.

The national urban pattern defined by 1900 hardly changed in the next four decades. Since 1940, there has been some realignment, as cities in the south and west have spurted forward around new technologies and energy resources. This growth has hardly, however, all been new invention. Los Angeles, the most astonishing urban prodigy of the twentieth century, already had more than four hundred thousand residents in 1910. Moreover, the manufacturing and commercial heartland of 1900 has continued to attract a substantial portion of the growth. The actual distribution is difficult, even retrospectively, to explain. The most powerful analysts settle for interpreting the pattern as the product of an almost random process in which, however, the larger the city, the greater its chances of growth.[3]

I have a special purpose in reversing the ordinary perception that the form of cities has been peculiarly unstable or changeful. The perception of change is rooted in observations of shifts in the location of activities within cities. Turning the perception on its head by focusing on the essentially conservative qualities of the whole urban system, opens a new array of problems and possibilities which are only beginning to appear on the public agenda.

There is now considerable talk about the wisdom and feasibility of constructing wholly new cities or of radically accelerating the growth rate of smaller urban areas.[4] There are some bits of legislation directed to this end, though not as yet much real action. Reston, Virginia, and Columbia, Maryland, the two most striking examples of new towns, have been studied, cited, and dreamed about until their bricks have turned into glass, and plan and reality have been hopelessly confused. A few proponents of the invention of substantially new cities have urged legislation which would restrict the growth of the largest urban centers. For them, the projection that by the year 2000, 187 million people, 60 per cent of the nation's population, will live in four urban agglomerations, is a projection of the apocalypse. For the most part, however, the advocates of redirection have confined themselves to the hope that new physical and socal amenities would attract residents, while business firms could be lured to new sites by industrial parks and tax advantages.

Many benefits have been ascribed to a redirective urban policy. Some proponents argue that when cities become very large, men press too hard on the natural ecology of regions in ways which are beyond the reach of even the most enlightened technological patching. Tidal marshes are covered over and river temperatures raised, with amplifying effects through the whole reach of the oceans. When ground water is exhausted, men can desalinate the seas. They cannot so easily replace the substratum of water in the geological and biological structure of the earth upon which they walk and build. Even local changes in climate may have effects which require more difficult adaptations than a new layer of clothing or a few extra B.T.U.'s of home heating.[5]

Engineers and designers have become interested in new settlements because they are prospectively open to innovative technologies and comprehensive planning.[6] In existing cities, improvements in public utilities characteristically occur at the margins of present systems. The result of innovation frequently is to increase the disparity between levels of performance in old sections and new. The poor, for example, are still dependent on removing all of their garbage by storing it for truck collection. The middle- and upper-classes enjoy the very substantial benefits of in-house garbage disposal units. A newly designed comprehensive system could eliminate these disparities and, at the same time, improve the level of sanitary services for even the currently most advantaged group. The physical separateness of new settlements is valued because it seems to remove them both from the institutional barriers to innovation in old sites and from the competition of less effective and equitable but, nevertheless, cheaper systems which have already been capitalized. There are better ways to move cars and wastes than the standard street grid and the sewers of most American cities. When the roads and pipes have already been paid for, however, its hard to imagine tearing them up to start over again.

Finally, the desire for redirection and the inhibition of mammoth urban concentrations has echoed an old complaint against cities. John Howard sees new cities and reinvigorated country towns as a relief from the "deepening submergence of the individual human being as the total numbers rise." "The degree to which population is massed," James Sundquist writes, "determines the amenity and congeniality of the whole environment. It affects their personal efficiency, their sense of community, their feelings about the relationship between man and nature, their individual and collective outlook on the world." [7]

Howard's and Sundquist's position has been placed in formal communications terms by Garrett Hardin. Hardin's formulation, though phrased in a plea for general population control, projects the issue of the intercity distribution of population into the center of a policy concerned with the expansion of communication and knowledge. "How many communication relationships (r)," he asks, are there in a subpopulation of x people?" His mathematically stated answer is $r = \dfrac{x(x-1)}{2}$, that is you communicate in a couplet with everyone but yourself. In a party with ten people, for example, r equals forty-five, that is, $\dfrac{10(10-1)}{2}$. Since each couplet requires a channel in both directions, the division by two may be ignored. In a large group, Hardin writes, it's convenient to consider that the channel requirements go up, "approximately as the square of the number of people in the group. This is a power function. We cannot escape this truth; we can merely evade it. We can shorten the time spent communicating with other people and thus adjust to a larger population. No doubt we do this in part: contrast a New York telephone conversation with a roadside chat in the Panhandle of Texas. But there is a limit to how much one can shorten the units of communication and still reach an understanding. Another way of evading the simple mathematical implications of this relationship is by withdrawing somewhat from the world, by erecting high psychic walls to keep at bay the ever-increasing hordes of people outside. This adjustment also we make. The larger the city, the less the neighborliness, the less willing people are to become involved with the problems of others." [8]

Would it be useful to create a host of smaller cities in order to break down psychic walls and to increase care and understanding? The customary way of answering the question is to examine the empirical evidence. Are small towns friendlier, more sharing, and more manageable places than big cities? Unfortunately, the evidence is ambiguous and depends in large part on the weighing of rival advantages and disadvantages. Moreover, a redirection of growth would have to reorganize so many functions in space that the evidence drawn from established systems is not entirely relevant. It does not follow that because large cities show more crime than small that we would be safer if we restricted metropolitan growth.

It may be useful to approach the question from another direction. The starting point for any serious redirective policy is to break the grip of the locational advantage of large urban centers. These advantages lie in the movement of both physical resources and information. Firms locate themselves in space to improve their access to markets, on one side of their activities, and to labor and raw materials on the other. Access, in every case, means something more than ease of transportation. A firm is close to its markets both when it can move its goods or services there cheaply and when it can perceive and respond to its customers' preferences, its competitors' behavior and new developments in its field of enterprise. Similarly, access to labor and raw materials includes elements of information and symbolic communication which are not measured in the accounting of freight schedules and relocation costs. Workers are not simply recruited by a firm at one moment in time and fixed as an entity in its production ledger. A firm, whether public or private, is concerned with the dynamics of the labor force which will allow it to expand its share of workers and to replace or retrain its present stock. Similarly, it buys knowledge of the price of buttons, the latest chemical synthesis, or the state of public opinion in a continuing market in which the new is constantly devaluing the old. Poor or out-of-date information is as much a handicap as sloppy workers or inferior materials.

Labor too, is concerned with the risks and advantages of varied environments. The characteristic pattern of national migration now is not farm to city, but up the urban hierarchy. Single industry towns are not so much embryonic cities as staging and training grounds for urban migrants who move on. Each move upward in scale, whatever its immediate uncertainties, reduces the risk of complete failure. If one job fails, there may be another in the same area. Moves into smaller cities, however, increase risks by breaking the link with larger labor markets.

A long list of innovations would be necessary to distribute over regional or national spaces the advantages to firms and workers in the intense clustering of work. The first communication items on the list are sufficient to establish the magnitude of the task:

- a national market for virtually all occupational groups. The communications system which would support this market would provide capacities for remote search procedures, interviewing, and hiring.
- a comparable market, with similar capacities, for housing. Within this market, the speed and ease with which transactions could be accomplished would have to be substantially increased.
- a daily list of current prices for specialized commodities and services, comparable to that now available for both money and bulk goods.
- comprehensive and evaluative bibliographic services in a wide variety of fields, and very fast document and data retrieval.

- an educational system capable of providing both adults and children with a uniformly high quality of training in virtually any subject or field, at virtually any site.

There are two contradictory reactions to a list such as this—both of which I recognize in myself. The first reaction is that these tasks are too difficult and illustrate the rationality of the power of established urban form. The difficulties are rooted initially in technical problems and costs. Such grand theorists of the future as Buckminster Fuller and Marshall McLuhan may conjure a world transformed into a scattered but still united village in which all knowledge is instantly available and in which work, school, entertainment, and shopping are all detached from reliance on place.[9] Actual workers in the vineyards of information and communication systems are generally less sanguine. The human brain is a remarkably varied and flexible instrument for the storage, retrieval, and analysis of information. A full natural language is an amazingly complex code for communication. Duplicating their capacities so as to increase access to information is both technically very difficult and financially very costly.

Some of the technical difficulties may be surmounted by building bigger and better machines. Others present conceptual problems which cannot be so easily overcome. Fifteen years ago there was a great deal of confidence that machines could be built which could translate one natural language into another. We discovered, however, that a finite machine could not manage to decipher the meanings in the infinite variety of natural sentences. Moreover, we did not even know fully how human beings manage this task. In a comparable fashion, there has been a great deal of enthusiasm for machine-prepared, stored, and printed bibliographies and data guides. The enthusiasm frequently pales when we realize that a bibliography represents one stable and uniform organization of knowledge in an array which theoretically includes an infinite number of organizational plans and practically (for real users) includes a very large number. Libraries where you poke around the shelves with knowledgeable people as guides are likely to continue to play important roles in any complex information system.[10]

Men who wrestle with these technical problems are undoubtedly impressed with their difficulty and reasonably confident that, if they could be solved, institutional barriers would be overcome. Social planners reverse this perspective. Technological difficulties seem subsidiary to organizational problems. The mayors of large central cities have already demonstrated less than wild enthusiasm for talk of the creation of new towns. A serious redirective policy would challenge the expectations for future profits of great numbers of landowners and businessmen. Each one of the particular communication innovations would threaten either the power or the accustomed modes of behavior of some established group. Since knowledge of current prices is a form of economic advantage, why should those who enjoy the privilege be willing to share it? Since a great library is a form of academic advantage, why should those who have them be interested in equalizing access to information? Many employers (ranging from university departments to department store shipping offices) hire new recruits who are friends of their old workers. The buddy system encourages newcomers to prove their worth so that friends will not be shamed. Old-timers, in turn, feel responsible for a novice's performance and help him along. Why should firms, except under conditions of market stringency, open their gates freely to strangers? Why should they want a completely open national labor market? [11]

There is an alternative to the pessimistic view of the requirements for innovation. It is possible to look at the list of tasks and to see in each of them an extension of an existing line of development. Most of the great communication innovations of the last century have been directed towards continental spaces. Farmers in Iowa and laborers in New York City can both laugh, cry, and yawn at the same television programs. Catalogue sales and automobile trips into the city have radically reduced the time lag between advanced fashions and popular adoption. The attempt to define urbanity as a set of attitudes peculiar to city dwellers has collapsed before this urbanization of the entire nation. High level managers, scientists, engineers, and professors already operate in a continental job market in which locational advantages are very weak. Existing computerized real estate services can substantially reduce their uncertainty in moving from one area to another.

The great force of the continental spread of information has, up to now, been to reduce the viability of small towns and the necessity of the enormous concentrations of metropolitan functions in New York and a very few other cities. On the one side, large firms in scattered sites have separated administrative from manufacturing functions and moved their corporate headquarters into cities. On the other side, regional metropolitan centers have assumed roles in the money and commercial markets which previously had been dominated by a few urban giants. The beneficiaries of diffusion—if benefit is measured by growth—seem to have been the middle-range cities in the size range between five hundred thousand and two million. Who is to say, however, that in the next wave of communications advance, the advantage may not move further downward? [12]

The communication requirements for redirection are more easily seen as extensions of current trends when they are drawn up into a list of specific technologies. For example, a group in Connecticut, encouraged by the National Academy of Engineering, is now focusing on shifting urban development to small towns in the northeastern portion of the state. The Academy's list of requirements has a reassuring ring of possibility, all the more so if you are not quite sure what all the technical terms mean:

1) Incoming broadband cable or microwave circuits which connect the town's businesses, industry, and government offices with their operations in other cities or countries. These are essentially dedicated point-to-point links.

2) Long-distance broadband circuits interconnecting the town's switched telephone and video-phone services with the corresponding switched services in other cities.

3) Common carrier broadband and narrow band services such as United States Postal Services, Western Union, and others for transmission of messages, printed material, data, etc. between towns and to other countries.

4) Incoming circuits for educational, cultural, and recreational pursuits. These would be:
   a) radio and television broadcast circuits both for private networks and public broadcasting
   b) two-way broadband educational television circuits interconnecting a small local campus with the region's central university

c) a broadband cable circuit as part of a national high-definition closed circuit television network bringing live Broadway, opera, concert, and sports productions to theaters especially geared for such presentations.[13]

The optimistic and pessimistic responses to the communication tasks are curiously similar in the perspective they offer on a redirective urban policy. The creation of a new array of small towns and cities may be designed to shape intimate environments, in which people can know one another and manage their local worlds. The chief requirement for such a creative act is, however, the broad sharing of local and private knowledge within large cities and the substitution of remote for direct personal communication. The dependence of the labor market upon friendship and familiarity must be further reduced by computerized personnel systems with remote terminals. Telephone and video conferences must cut deeply into the role of lunchtime meetings and informal but closed chit-chat in business decision making.

The paradox of the redirective position—that intimacy in one place can only be bought with mechanization in another—should not be surprising. Only the illusion of a spatial model of community could support a belief that the communication requirements of a national society might be reduced by shifting people from one city to another. Hardin's x^2 remains the same if Connecticut grows in its central spine or in the northeast. If you reduce the capacities of big city streets, corridors, and restaurants you must replace them with wires and airwaves.

Discovery of this paradox does not imply that a redirective urban policy, with its many purported benefits, is unwise. But the costs now seem very high for very uncertain benefits.

I am also wary of a political linkage between communications policy and urban redirection. There is a common and specious assumption that proponents of similar technologies share similar values, as if computers, remote xerography, and television lines describe one —and only one—society. In fact, the same technologies may serve a wide variety of ends and be linked in wholly opposite directions. A technological effort to duplicate urban advantages in scattered sites

51

must necessarily focus on the communication requirements of business firms. There is also an understandable tendency to copy the élite cultural amenities of the big city, as expressed in the National Academy's concern with the closed circuit transmission of live Broadway, opera, concert and sports productions.

In established cities, where the networks for business communication and live music and theatre already exist, there is no need to create them anew. Communications policy may there concentrate on the extension of these networks or the creation of new alternatives. The social direction of the policy may be downward and democratic rather than élitist. Overall, I suspect, the idea of a national urban policy to redirect growth is a distraction from the task of building congenial communities.

It may be, of course, that current discussions of a redirective urban policy will only amount to a small hill of beans. At best, we may shape guidelines for the coordinated development of the urban fringe. The exercise of exploring the large-scale relationships between communication and space nevertheless sets the issue of interaction and residential integration in a useful framework. Can the problematic benefits of the reorganization of whole cities in space be more certainly achieved by the internal reordering of existing cities? Can communities of understanding be extended by the integration of small areas?

The urban hierarchy developed in the nineteenth century has been amazingly conserved. The internal pattern of each of the established cities has, however, been dramatically transformed. A succession of improvements in transportation which date well back into the nineteenth century first expanded the total size of the former "walking cities," and then progressively reduced the necessary density of development. Cities largely built in the automobile age show this reduction of density most clearly but the same pattern is apparent in older cities. The cores of New York, Boston, Philadelphia, and Baltimore are less dense than they were in 1900 and their suburbs widely spread. New fringe developments in Boston, for example, use more land per house than similar growth in the new suburbs of Los Angeles.[14]

The spatial expansion of cities and the reduction of densities has stretched the grain of housing segregation. Little segregated clusters, like dots on a flaccid balloon, were pulled out by the expansion of the city to cover broader areas. Most of the effects attributed to segregation may be explained by this simple expansive effect. There have, however, been two additional forces operating which the balloon image does not reveal. First, the relative location of social classes has been altered. Gideon Sjoberg describes a preindustrial city in which élite groups lived close to the center and the poor trailed out behind them. While there are still very important élite enclaves near the center of the most older cities, the general pattern reverses the traditional arrangement.[15] The reversal becomes important when political boundaries are fixed and the central portions of urban areas are left with a shortage of high-income residents.

The second force is the selective quality of the improvement in transportation. Overall, the opening of new metropolitan land has increased segregation. Here and there, however, special locational advantages have not been touched by the miracle of the automobile. Such large upper-class areas as the Philadelphia Main Line provide little enclaves for the clerks, domestic workers, policemen, and janitors it requires. Similarly, executives and professionals in most cities have preserved or reclaimed areas within walking distance of their center city offices.

The shape of urban expansion and the segregation of populations cannot simply be attributed to snobbery or a preference for "one's own kind." Through most of the nineteenth century, the reduction of urban densities was conceived as the major tool of reform policy. Trolley cars, subways, buses, 'el's, and automobiles were instruments of opportunity.[16] The decision to invest heavily in transportation had the effect, however, of reversing the older process in which established sites were reclaimed for new uses. Instead, a population with increasing wealth and new or newly effective tastes has found it cheaper to build afresh than to tear down and reconstruct.

The cost calculus sometimes, of course, works in favor of rebuilding. Since World War II, virtually every major city has found that it pays to displace old centrally located business facilities with new and to put luxury apartment houses where tenements and walk-ups stood.

Urban renewal in this form, while it is glittering and frequently controversial, is, however, only a small wrinkle on the larger urban explosion.

If transportation had not substantially reduced urban distances, then entire sections of cities, rather than small central areas, would be repeatedly rebuilt. New homeowners would either rehabilitate old houses or tear them down and build from scratch on the old site rather than buying in suburban subdivisions. The building industry would be adapted to this process, including in its range of practice substantial experience at constructing new dwellings for lower-income groups. Instead, of course, the industry is adapted to new construction for the middle and upper classes. Old structures remain standing because it does not pay to remove them. Improved heating systems and fire protection prevent them from even burining down as often as in the past. The result of these influences is that the older structures of the city are more obsolete in relation to current standards and technologies than they were in 1850. Their wiring, their plumbing, their room design and yard space—all are obstacles to the social integration of neighborhoods.

The pattern of segregation which has emerged from the complex pull of many forces is the subject of a great deal of scholarly contention and serious research. Certainly, the pattern cannot simply be described by a contrast between cities and suburbs, poor cousins and rich. The suburbs have taken such a large portion of the urban population that they can no longer be cast in the unique image of havens for the substantial middle class. There are, and have been for a very long time, a wide range of suburban types. Indeed, the outer edges of cities characteristically house some of the poorest segments of the population.

The actual pattern appears something like the confused image projected through three colored transparencies, two broadly similar for most cities, the third, idiosyncratic. The first transparency describes broad axes radiating from the urban center and segregated according to income, education, and occupation. The second overlay pictures a set of rings. The inner circles are inhabited by small families, usually young couples or older people whose children are already grown. The densities are high, apartments common, and renters more frequent than owners. In the outer rings, live large families in their own houses. The wives are at home. The final transparency varies in its pattern from city to city and defies generalization. It portrays the segregation of blacks from whites and ethnic clusterings which have spurned the seductions of class.[17]

With three different transparencies, each segregating a different dimension, discussions of integration take on a complexity that is rarely acknowledged. Treating race and ethnicity as a single dimension and confining statements to the simple form, "I want more integration," there are still seven different possible affirmative strategies:

- integrate the axes by mixing classes together.
- integrate the rings by mixing households of different ages and life style together.
- integrate the enclaves by mixing races and ethnic groups.
- integrate rings with axes by encouraging people of different ages and life styles but similar income or education to live near one another.
- integrate rings with enclaves by providing housing for a variety of household types within the enclaves, or scattering racial and ethnic groups through the rings, without, however, altering the class bases of segregation.
- integrate axes with enclaves by providing housing for a variety of classes within the enclaves, or, more characteristically, encouraging racial and ethnic groups to scatter through the city, buying space wherever their incomes allow.
- integrate the entire city, so that each neighborhood includes members of every class, racial, ethnic, and demographic group.

There is a special political dynamic for each one of these strategies. In many well-to-do suburban areas of single family homes, the erection of luxury high-rise or garden apartments is a source of local conflict. Similarly, the scarcity of large apartments and houses for young families with several children is one of the most pressing prob-

55

lems for ethnic leaders who want to preserve the segregation of their enclaves. An Italian neighborhood will not persist if its first generation of successful college graduates cannot find suitable homes within its boundaries.

In addition to their separate dimensions, the integrative strategies are also intertwined. The scattering of racial and ethnic groups through the whole city, often leaves segregated clusters of the elderly poor as the heirs of the old enclave. Zoning, designed to inhibit apartment houses in the midst of a residential district, may force a racial, ethnic, or class change, when no buyers can be found for old single family homes. The short term result may be integration, but in the long run the whole neighborhood may shift to reinforce the segregated pattern.

Each of the integrative strategies generates conflict; each conflict, its own body of critical analysis. Some of this analysis has a short life span. The first suburban explosion after World War II led to a cultural critique of the fertile subdivisions where the sun never shone on a gray head. Lo and behold, the suburbs aged, apartments were built for older folks, and few youngsters grew up thinking that the whole world was under forty.[18]

The abiding issues, and the ones which have continued to provoke concern with the pattern of social communication, are class and race.

It is strange, after all the bitter words of the past, how little can be said about the removal of all legal and institutional barriers to racial integration. The symbols of legitimacy have been thoroughly stripped from exclusionary public policies and private behavior. Poles who would block black purchasers, without, however, outbidding them, command no more sympathy than wealthy Protestants who impose barriers to Jewish buyers.

Commitment to this equality of access is not contingent upon an evaluation of its direct results. It may be, for example, that if black buyers were able to buy homes anywhere in a city and chose to do so, several very severe problems would result. The class segregation of the ghetto would be increased with a resulting loss of both political leadership and professional and business services. The new migrants might as easily prove to be "class traitors" as "empathetic ambassadors" and the level of effective repression of ghetto interests might be raised.

(The era of this "might," may, of course, have passed. It expresses as a future possibility, the pattern against which E. Franklin Frazier inveighed in his study, *The Black Bourgeoisie*.) [19]

There is no way, in the name of either conservatism or social planning, to restrict access in order to preclude any of these effects. Social adaptation will have to be achieved within the context of open opportunity.

There are a great many serious problems surrounding strategies for measuring and achieving openness, but the end itself has a sacred quality (which, of course, increases the ire of those who do not share it). The only controversy about goals which seriously threatens public practices and institutions relates not to color but to class. Even middle-class black neighborhoods are outraged by suggestions that poor people deserve a place in their residential sun.

There are three distinct arguments in favor of class integration. The first and simplest is that it is the only feasible way of achieving racial mixture. This argument is not entirely fair. Virtually every major American city has more lower-income whites than blacks. These whites already carry what is perceived as the major burden of racial integration. If other arguments did not intervene, and if the game seemed worth the candle, it would be possible to pronounce racial but not class integration as a goal of public policy.

The second and third arguments do, however, intervene. The second describes the class integration of small areas as a major instrument for the equalization of public services; the third, as an instrument of social communication and expanded understanding and empathy. These two arguments are not totally unrelated, but it is important to preserve their distinctiveness in order to deal honestly with those who oppose them.

Imagine for a moment that political units enter a market place to buy tax-producing agents called citizens. Since a wealthy taxpayer is worth more than a poor one, the unit has every reason to bid to keep him within its territory. In a segregated setting, wealthy sections should receive better schools, cleaner streets, fuller recreational facilities, and more thorough police protection than low income areas.

This imagined market place does not fully describe the actual pattern in which services are distributed. Practical politics, democratic norms, and the need to share many facilities lead to violations of the rational allocation of public amenities. The market model is, however, amazingly powerful. Almost every study of police protection, recreation, sanitation and education in American cities reveals a pattern in which wealthy neighborhoods or suburbs are better served than poor ones. The market model even makes sense of apparently anomolous decisions by some small cities and suburbs which skimp on schools or other services as if they wanted to discourage middle-class residents. In fact, they may only be accommodating themselves to the realities of the market. In a competitive situation some firms—or cities—may rationally decide to specialize in lower income "customers." [20]

The major egalitarian response to this inequality of public services is to expand the boundary of the tax unit. In the past, even reform politicians have insisted that low-income housing had to be replaced with high-income units in order to hold wealthy residents in older central cities. However, if taxes were raised on a metropolitan basis, or by the state—or even by the federal government—then there would be nowhere for the rich to run. Then the poor could no longer be asked to subsidize the rich.

There are important limits to this strategy of fiscal equalization. The connection between private wealth and public benefits is so deep that it reasserts itself in the face of even good-willed efforts at reform. Several cities have largely eliminated class differences in school facilities or district-by-district educational expenditures. Nevertheless, the ordinary movement of experienced or ambitious teachers to successful school environments contrives subtly to reallocate resources.

Even if teachers did not move, equalization of expenditures in education and most other systems would deal with only a portion of the connection between private and public advantages. Most public services are parts of larger systems in which private and governmental expenditures overlap and complement one another. Uniform street garbage collection in two districts, one with home disposal units, the other without, does not equalize cleanliness. Uniform school expenditures in two districts, one in which the parents talk "school talk," the other in which they don't, hardly equalizes opportunity and achievement.

It is possible, of course, to go beyond formal equality in expenditures or facilities, publicly compensating for a lack of private expenditures. There are a great many government policies designed with this goal, though most are neatly balanced by advantages to upper- and middle-income groups. Moreover, large concentrations of the poor make it very difficult substantively to equalize many services and opportunities and raise the cost beyond practical political imagination.

Substantive equalization, therefore, often appears to require a change in the class mix of small areas—rather than simply sharing money—in a manner which effects the operations of service systems themselves.[21] The requirements for mixture depend upon the actual bundle of amenities which is to be redistributed. There is no need to integrate every block if it is a school system which is to be shared. On the other side, however, garbage trucks have frequently managed to leave back alleys untouched while they sanitize the main streets. Equal sanitation and public maintenance will require a finer grain of residential integration than education.

The problems and possibilities associated with either the movement of money or the movement of people deserve very careful examination. I have discussed them here only to point out that the redistribution of benefits through the reorganization of urban space, though it deals directly with class relationships, is only indirectly related to intergroup communication. It may be that people who live in a cleaner and less violent environment, closer to parks and with better schools, will get a different message about the legitimacy of their society or the salience of opportunity than the residents of present ghettos. It may also be that they will be impressed into a passive and deferential role which would hardly be conducive to an open sharing of experience. In either case, both the shape of class interaction and the reality of opportunity will depend on acts which go far beyond the range of a spatial policy.

There is an argument for class integration which goes beyond redistribution to speak directly to problems of communication. An old and prestigious vision of the city describes it as peculiarly the site of variety, contact between classes, and extended social understanding. Of late, this vision—as expressed most powerfully in Jane Jacob's picture of Hudson Street in Greenwich Village—has fastened upon the integrated neighborhood as an educational environment developing both understanding and a commitment to democracy.[22]

There are several problems with this vision. To paraphrase a well-known children's book, "How small is small?" Quite obviously, the nation itself is fully integrated. Most major metropolitan areas have a similar full measure of rich and poor living together. Subparts of the area, such as a central city or suburb, characteristically include a skewed sample of the total population. The sample becomes more and more segregated as the size of the area is reduced. Blocks include a narrower range of income than census tracts or neighborhoods; households narrower than blocks.

The appropriate scale of residential integration to encourage communication has to be defined first by the access of individuals to one another. Accessibility, as a potential for interaction, depends upon the capacities of the linking channels of communication—whether they be streets, bus routes, telephone lines, or television signals. Most of the arguments for residential integration are rooted in the imagery of a walking population. As a matter of fact, of course, the largest part of the population in most cities goes to work by car and can move across metropolitan spaces with great ease. Boris Pushkarev of the New York Regional Plan Association has played a little game with this fact. A man could walk in the dense Manhattan of 1850 at about three miles per hour. He could drive in the spacious outer suburbs of New York in 1960 at about thirty miles an hour. In both cases, ten minutes of travel time would bring him into possible contact with twenty-five thousand people.[23]

Without pushing this observation too hard—the nature of the contacts are not entirely comparable—it does suggest that there are alternatives to residential integration in transportation and communication policies. Most of this volume deals with remote media used in new ways to extend public understanding. Transportation should also, however, be improved to open the city to inspection and comprehension. The poor are the only group in the population not yet to have entered fully the automobile age.[24] Their isolation might be substantially reduced by developing smaller and cheaper modes of individualized transport. The new autos may be small, they may be rented, they may, hopefully, be kinder to the atmosphere—but we need more cars on the road.

Access as a reality, rather than simply as a potential, depends upon the structure and significance of the tasks which bring people together. When there is nothing to be done, men who live close together may never meet; where important goals are to be achieved, distance recedes as a barrier.

Most of the conceptions of the cosmopolitan neighborhood focus on the task commonly called "neighboring." There is an extensive body of scholarly research and writing on neighboring behavior. A good deal of it, encouraged by the dream of social integration, is designed to measure the range and depth of interclass contacts. The overwhelming conclusion of this research is that the task of getting along with the people who live close to you depends on a delicate balance of reciprocal obligations and duties. Neighbors must be able to pay one another back for services performed in short-term emergencies, in confirming parental demands upon children, and in supporting norms of public behavior. This required reciprocity ordinarily requires that neighbors either be very similar in income and values or that they develop ways of insulating themselves from one another.[25]

Propinquity as a channel, neighboring as communicative exchange, have very special capacities. Casual intimacy between adults—watching children play, borrowing sugar, seeing each other on the street—can erode initially perceived differences and lead to friendship and understanding across barriers of race and ethnicity. These barriers, if they are not compounded by differences in education, income, and occupational experience, rarely represent important differences in values or behavior.

Class—as an amalgam of education, income, and occupation—does generate differences which are real and persistent. At work, people cope with these differences because the rewards for cooperation are so desired and so immediate. In political parties, they also cope—again the rewards of victory are compelling. At home or on the block, there is very little reason to want to bother. It's hard to negotiate over differences, to insulate from threat, to understand the strange and unexpected. Successful neighboring does not seem worth these difficulties.

Richard Sennett in *The Uses of Disorder: Personal Identity and City Life* [26] reiterates the vision of class integration while addressing the limited rewards of conventional neighboring. His solution, however, only reinforces my own estimate that spatial realignment is an unlikely program for the expansion of social understanding.

Sennett's major complaint is directed towards low-density upper-income suburbs, which he describes as attempts to shape "purified communities," without diversity or conflict. The bitter fruit of such communities, reaped again and again as new generations shape new settlements, are adults who have not learned the skills of mature accommodation with reality. They preserve an adolescent image that a principle—or a world it shapes—is either all right or all wrong.

There are a great many empirical and analytical holes in Sennett's suburban description. He certainly underestimates the variety of suburban forms, exaggerates their homogeneity, and misses entirely the riskful interclass encounters undertaken by striving, upwardly mobile middle-class Americans. Difficulties in a problem statement do not, however, damn the solutions.

Sennett's solution ingeniously begins with children. They are the least mobile portion of the population and cannot use automobiles at their own command to overcome space. Their diverse "neighbors" have to be casually available in the streets of integrated neighborhoods. The street life of children cannot, however, be successfully detached for long from the web of adult connections. In order to bring adults together, Sennett specifies a set of tasks which go beyond casual neighboring. He proposes that a broad range of city functions be localized and debureaucratized. Zoning and eminent domain would both be abolished. If neighbors didn't like a new land use, they could picket and protest, but they could not preclude it by law. New public facilities would be locally planned rather than shaped by professionals in a downtown office. The police would no longer help solve interpersonal or intergroup conflicts. Parties to conflict would have to manage for themselves, perhaps with the assistance of their neighbors. Schools, similarly, would be locally run.

Sennett's proposal for "survival communities" is admittedly a sketch plan, knowingly elliptical in its discussion of the connection between neighborhoods, the role of central institutions, and the organization of real estate markets to generate the densities he desires. It's certainly possible, even in sketch form, not to like the plan. It would be enormously time-consuming; would risk, in eliminating impersonal bureaucracies, a plague of personal governance, and would be very rough on children, stripping them of the shield of the system of social stratification.

I am concerned, however, with a less sharply evaluative judgment. Most large cities already have areas, usually close to the center, which roughly conform to Sennett's image. Generalizing the life styles of these areas to larger populations would require a vast initial change in images of social life, preferences, and strategies. Political institutions would have to be reconstructed. The only way to use a spatial program as a direct instrument of expanded understanding is to precede it with a remote and relatively risk-free sharing of experiences and ideas. Without that sharing, Sennett's survival communities would be so much pie in the sky; with it, they might be unnecessary.

The next three chapters deal with modes of expanding understanding. I begin, with a small taste for paradox, with the one communications network in which spatial reorganization has been shown to generate new understanding.

FOUR

INTEGRATED EDUCATION: *Purposes*

Researchers have worked hard to demonstrate that heterogeneous neighborhoods encourage varied interactions and broad social understanding. Their efforts have not been rewarded with any very general or persuasive findings. In the field of education, in contrast, studies of class integration have generated a powerful scholarly consensus.

Lower-class children, the consensus holds, learn more effectively when they are taught together with a majority of wealthier peers. Upper-class children do not suffer from this contact, at least as their performance is measured by tests of very general academic skills. When children and adults who have experienced integrated education are compared with those who have been wholly segregated through school they appear to be less prejudiced. They tend to judge individuals rather than groups and are willing to risk intergroup contacts. No existing program of segregated but improved education has come close to achieving the academic and attitudinal benefits of integration.

This does not rule out the possibilities of such compensatory improvement in the future. Reasonable cost estimates, however, mark compensation without integration as almost unimaginably expensive.

There are, of course, differences within the broad consensus. Studies vary somewhat, for example, in their assessment of the independent importance of racial, as compared with class, integration. These research differences are not terribly important, however, since the most optimistic accounts of the significance of racial mixture, suggests that blacks only experience modest benefits from integration with poor whites. Since the Negro middle class is quite small, class integration of poor blacks will require racial integration as well.[1]

In hundreds of small cities and rural areas, the policy implications of this scholarly consensus are fairly easy to pursue. Though many whites may protest, the framework of segregation is highly vulnerable to legal attack. In the largest cities, however, there are very extended areas which are either black or poor. In these settings, the mandate to integrate challenges the boundaries of school districts, the ordinary methods of distributing children in facilities, and a long array of popular preferences and educational norms. In small cities, these same issues may be raised. Skillful political leaders however, may, if they desire, focus attention on the legal imperative to integrate, on the clear feasibility of integration, and on the relatively minor character of the change. However abstractly questions may be posed, contestants must answer immediate questions: Shall a new central high school be built? a court order complied with? a superintendent supported?

In the largest cities, in contrast, the debate over integration characteristically deals with vague statements of intent, experiments which either were never designed to succeed or could never be generalized, and dreams of a reconstructed future in which the constraints of the present drop away. After a few experiences with this debate it is easy to catch a virulent case of battle fatigue. This fatigue was expressed in the widespread sense in the late 1960s that integration was dead as an issue. In fact, of course, it was very much alive outside of New York, Los Angeles, Chicago, Philadelphia, Detroit, and Cleveland.

The frustrations of big city integration are not entirely wasted. These frustrations have forced a reexamination of the goals and structures of American education. Long-established relations between teachers and parents, teachers and students, school boards and neighborhood associations, have all been challenged; basic teaching methods and philosophy reevaluated. All of this rethinking may appear frequently as a way of doing complexly and tomorrow what could be done simply today. There is really no way, however, of adapting educational institutions to new demands without a great deal of talk and mental experimentation. We tend to change the world in our heads a thousand times before we risk altering it in practice.

I have two purposes in entering the tangle of educational rethinking. The first is to clarify statements about goals and educational systems which impede serious communication between groups. It is particularly important that the limits of the public commitment to equality be honestly stated and understood. The second purpose is to suggest new communication strategies which may stretch these limits in the largest cities.

The educational advocates of race and class integration have created a history which legitimates their aspirations and strategies. Through the course of the nineteenth and most of the twentieth century, this history begins, the major goal of American education was to create a set of institutions accessible to all, in which the opportunity to learn was freely available. This goal was not always reached but it was a major impetus to action. Segregated school systems were legalized only because of the willingness of the courts to accept them as consistent with the goal of equal access.

In the last two decades, the goal of equality has been redefined. Equal opportunity cannot be measured by the formal availability of educational institutions. The only appropriate measure of equality is a similar distribution of achievement in major subgroups of the population. This rephrasing is not really a shift in goals. Increasing sociological sophistication has simply made it impossible to accept a facade of formal accessibility without real equality of opportunity. Genuinely unequal opportunities are incompatible with democratic theory—hence the shift in definitions. In order to equalize opportunities it may be necessary to move children across space. The resistance to busing has no standing in law and no historic tradition.

The great American tradition is not the neighborhood school but the common school in which all classes meet.[2]

It is hard to quarrel with the items in this history. I certainly wish that they were all true. Overall, however, the propositions are marked with the taint of the lawyer's brief. They are designed to win the case by cutting the historical and ideological grounds out from under the opposition. Unfortunately, this strategy is inappropriate in politics. Political persuasion usually depends upon finding a retrospective path which validates an opponent's present stance but opens futures which he has not yet imagined. The debater's victory is a hollow triumph since it does not provide a firm ground on which two parties can pridefully walk together.

An alternative history which might provide a basis for agreement would begin with two operative demands which have shaped American education in the last century and a half. The first, and most important, has been the demand for a highly trained work force; the second, for a devoted citizenry.

The demand for workers should not be interpreted solely as the narrow wish of manufacturers for skilled workingmen and engineers. It also includes the requests of theoretical physicists, newspaper publishers, physicians, and city planners for new professional recruits. The appropriate response to this demand has always been a matter of great uncertainty, since decisions have to be made now about the appropriate range of available skills in the distant future. This uncertainty has led to divisions in the ranks of professional school people who have borne the major responsibility for manpower planning. One group—it hardly matters here whether we are focusing on 1850 or 1970—has consistently warned against a too narrow interpretation of the skill demands of the future. This group has usually phrased its task as *education* rather than *training*. A second group has been quite willing to train. Its proposals, institutions, and human products have always been very practical, applied, and, in the eyes of the educators, both restricted and quickly obsolete.

The division among schoolmen has paralleled a conflict in the larger pool of public demanders. One group, including both businessmen and university professors, has constantly worried that the schools would produce too many aspirants for élite roles. Hence the image of the unemployable intellectual and the fastiduous white-collar snob who would not do the work of the world. The curriculum of the educators, whether it emphasized theoretical science or humanistic culture, has been derided as wasteful and unnecessary. On the other side, educators have insisted that the schools were training for yesterday and were pervaded by a narrow vocationalism.[3]

The actual shape of the American educational system has been a product of these divisions within large publics and within the ranks of professionals. The enormous long-term expansion of skill requirements has allowed the educators to control the symbolic hierarchy of schools and roles. Theirs is the power and the glory. The trainers are not, however, without influence in their own realms. Just as some elementary and high schools knowingly train students for working-class jobs, some colleges and graduate schools pride themselves that their students are practical and down-to-earth—none of the fancy, theoretical stuff for them.

The major feature of the educational system, which obscures this intended inequality and reinforces the myth of equalization, stems from a simple demographic fact. The social élite of one generation has always been too small to fill all the élite or skilled roles in the next generation. The children of the merchant bankers of 1820 could not fill all of the jobs at the top of manufacturing firms in 1880; the lathe operators and construction foremen of 1880 could not produce enough engineers to meet the requirements of 1920.[4]

There is a recurrent folk story about the manner in which skilled groups have resolved this demographic dilemma. The childless manufacturer visits the orphans' home, selects a successor, and trains him for leadership. Variations of the story place the site of selection as the front office where the apprentice clerks toil or the crowded street where the runaway horse is stopped.

Realistically, of course, the major responsibility for recruiting the élites of the next generation falls upon the schools. They have gone about their job by initially training large numbers of students, from whom the chosen few, at each step of the educational ladder, are selected. This dual process of expansion and selection generates most of the major tensions surrounding the educational system. As more people complete high school and the withdrawal (or drop-out) rate declines, the value of a high school diploma is depreciated. As school success at progressively more specialized levels becomes more central to occupational success, the fear of uncontrollable downward mobility is accentuated.[5]

The design of the educational system which responded to the demographic dilemma was simple enough. Wealthy groups developed unique educational institutions which fed into desired occupational roles. Through most of the nineteenth and early twentieth centuries, the number of individuals in any one small geographic locality who could support a differentiated institution was, however, very small. Differentiation required gathering the children of wealthy parents from a large region and educating them away from home in a boarding school or university. This tiny creaming from the top of local social structures left most children to be educated together in common institutions. In the late nineteenth century, the most widely shared institution was probably the primary and grammar school as the drop-out rate increased rapidly with the onset of adolescence. The subsequent growth of secondary school enrollments, coupled with the diffusion of populations in space, reversed this pattern. Children were now more likely to attend socially homogeneous lower schools and socially heterogenous high schools.[6]

In the course of more than a century, the common school was invested with an egalitarian ideology which wrapped the institution in a mantle of moral meaning and value. This ideology served very important purposes. It particularly was a weapon against élite attempts to defend family prerogatives by restricting access into the common schools.[7] It was also undemocratic for wealthy Protestants to keep Jews or Catholics out of colleges; for plumbers to restrict apprenticeships to their own sons.

The egalitarian ideology—like most grand ideas—never fully represented the preferences of the general population. In a society where great numbers of people with modest incomes aspired to give their own children a uniquely advantageous educational head start, it was economically efficient to educate these children together. Though most parents desired unequal chances for their children, few could afford the luxury of a class-segregated school. As incomes rose, however, the effective demand for these schools soared. The demand was even given an additional push by the extension of common schooling to the high school. As long as only the elementary grades were integrated, there was little chance that a middle-class child would marry across the tracks. Beyond puberty, the risks were greater.

The response to this demand is apparent in the pattern of American education: class-differentiated suburban districts and a new flowering of private schools.

This pattern is often very difficult to reconcile with democratic theory. When the pattern is threatened, however, defenders are able to articulate a rationale which must be considered very seriously. We assume in such a society as that of the United States that in the next generation we will need both more knowledge and more knowledgeable men and women than we have today. How, we constantly ask ourselves, will we develop this knowledge? How and whom shall we train?

The easiest way to answer these questions is to resolve to build on existing strengths: cultivate those institutions which currently generate knowledge, encourage those students who are successful from the very beginning of their school careers. In most circumstances, this easy path looms as the most rational and most efficient, for its direct beneficiaries and for the nation as a whole. Unfortunately, it also clashes with the goal of equal opportunity since existing strengths are rooted in the existing pattern of social differences.

This relationship between opportunities in the past and those in the future goes beyond the ability of one generation to transmit its financial wealth to another. If you list American occupations on a chart from high to low status, there are a few dimensions of work itself which vary closely with status and with income. Tasks at the bottom of the list require workers to manipulate less information and choose between fewer alternatives than those at the top. In each status, men develop a sense of the total organizational effort in which they are involved and develop strategies to protect themselves and to manipulate others. As you move up the list, the self-protection or enhancement is, however, likely to involve the manipulation of more resources and more players. The manual laborer, to use a stereotypic

71

example, learns how to fake it; the junior executive plays office politics; the company president reorganizes his staff. The larger strategies require an extended ability to imagine how others see their situation and to alter one's own behavior accordingly.

The hierarchy of work is riddled with exceptions to this progression. At several different levels, men who ratify decisions have less power and less authority than their subordinates who decide between major alternatives and structure the process of choice. The commonly granted prestige of white-collar occupations obscures the greater autonomy and complexity of many blue-collar tasks. In any particular job, the attitudes and skills which lead to success may be very different from those I have described and may be less transferable to the next generation. A salesman, for example, may not be able to replicate his drive in his children. Finally, in sports, family life, churches, politics, and voluntary organizations men whose work trains them to obey may learn to lead.

These exceptions to the general pattern warn against stereotyping individuals and provide room for social change and individual mobility. The exceptions end, however, by emphasizing the enormous force of the general pattern. Attitudes and skills which are rewarded at work are generalized to other dimensions of life and are a major input into the training of children. Middle and upper-class children, both before and during the school experience, are advantaged by parental efforts to train them to deal with complex information and to examine a wide range of alternatives in response to a problem. The training is based on the parents' perceptions of what succeeds at work. The parents may make a mistake in their perceptions or may not be able to act upon them. They are, however, more likely to be right than wrong about the environment they encounter every day.[8]

We have every reason to believe that children learn their lessons. As you move up the social ladder, children tend to become more skilled in their basic use of language and in their array of communication skills. Their vocabularies grow larger, so that they can specify distinctly a greater array of items and attributes. While the number of basic patterns in speech may not vary very much from child to child, there are distinct gradients in the flexibility with which patterns are used and related to one another. Skilled speakers, who tend to come from the top of the social scale, have a variety of grammatical devices to subordinate ideas to one another. This allows them to keep more relationships in mind simultaneously and, consequently, to generate more permutations of an initial set of relationships and to select alternatives from a wider universe of choice. They also seem to be more skilled in shifting from one perspective to another, putting themselves in someone else's shoes.[9]

The relationship between linguistic skill and social class is far from absolute. (Moreover, skill takes on different meanings in diverse settings. An advantage in one arena may be disabling in another). The relationship is, however, strong enough to reinforce existing class structures and to perpetuate inequalities from one generation to the next. It is always cheaper and easier for schools to supplement middle-class parental efforts than to duplicate them in all strata of the population. Even if narrow self-interest and institutional barriers did not intervene, it is likely that the costs of equal educational opportunity would impose heavy burdens on preferences widely held in our society. The rich are not disposed to pay for it; the poor may not be willing to suffer it. This does not mean that equality should not be an important goal; only that thoroughgoing equalization is an extremely costly and unlikely policy.

I began this alternative history of American education by specifying two shaping demands in the last century and a half. The first was for the creation of a more highly trained work force. This demand generated the class-integrated school as a practical solution to a demographic and financial dilemma. The second demand has been for the training of citizens.

Citizenship is a broad blanket. In the nineteenth and twentieth centuries it has covered at least three related goals. The first and most important is the creation in the student body of a primary set of identifications as Americans, uniquely linked to the nation-state by a network of reciprocal obligations and loyalties. The schools tried to distract attention from all personal, family, and group histories which might shape alternative identities. Positively, they tried to create a common set of cultural heroes, a common set of founders, and a

73

common general history. Even more critically, they usually suppressed immigrant languages and insisted on the exclusive use of English as a medium of national expression.[10] Under pressure from immigrant or racial groups, specialized histories or languages have, from time to time, been added to the curriculum. Consistent with the larger goal, the addition usually is designed to accentuate the vitality of the common framework. Immigrants and blacks are acknowledged for their contributions; languages are revived as foreign after the children and grandchildren of immigrants have safely forgotten them.

The second goal adds flesh and content to the idea of citizenship and links it to productive engagement in the world of work. The citizen, most schools have been insisting since the early nineteenth century, is cooperative, law-abiding, and respectful of duly constituted authority. He accepts the framework of social and economic institutions, disdains radicalism, and dislikes conflict.[11]

The final goal of citizenship programs is to encourage each child to recognize the brotherhood of man and the worth of the individual. This goal is usually expressed in a vague, deeply-felt, but somewhat saccharine rhetoric. The goal may be clarified, at some cost in feeling, by a cold social-scientific translation. I take the usual rhetoric to mean that every child should learn that certain qualities are distributed across the whole social scale and certain rights are defined as universally applicable. Sensing what is general, children must also come to understand what is variable and particular. They must learn first to evaluate stereotypes and generalizations critically. Wealthy children must be opened to the discovery that some of the poor may be brighter and more capable than themselves. Blacks and whites must be able to form friendships across socially prescribed racial lines.

The complement of this critical perspective is an awareness of the uses of stereotypes and generalizations. Developing social understanding and communication skills depends upon comprehending that a man may indeed behave as he does because he is rich or black, Indian or Portuguese, a ditch-digger or a lawyer.[12]

This final goal of citizenship programs is curiously both the most powerful and the most fragile of the three. It is powerful because it associates citizenship with social knowledge rather than a restricted set of attitudes. It is fragile because the demand for this knowledge is more specialized than its partisans would happily allow. Most people —again it does not matter whether the focus is on 1850 or 1970— have been interested in developing a perception of the relationship between personal attributes and social position. For the most part, however, their eyes have either looked around them or upwards in social space. They have wanted to train their children in the appropriate norms of their own or of some more prestigious group. Knowledge downward was either of low priority or was positively threatening.[13]

The threat could either be very immediate in form of the possibility of a bad marriage or it might take the shape of a nagging suspicion that the life of the lower classes was dangerously attractive: free, irresponsible, and promiscuous.[14]

The goal of social understanding is the only citizenship statement which explicitly directs the design of educational systems towards class integration. Most people's preferences, however, shape this design so that individual schools rarely include a full social range. The only constituency which cares enough about this goal to value downward-looking integration is composed largely of a portion of the economic and intellectual élite which sees a broad social imagination as important attributes of its own position. This group wants to integrate Harvard, Yale, Princeton, Wesleyan, and the public school systems of Evanston and Berkeley. It is ready to consent that its own social isolation may be a form of spiritual deprivation. Unfortunately, this group is relatively small, relatively wealthy, and extremely demanding in its educational expectations. It has no reason to be tolerant of inept educational processes.

Its intolerance is understandably compounded by the very breadth of its educational expectations. Members of this group want their children to learn not simply what it is like to be poor or to be black, but also to be Indian or Russian, to have lived in 1800 or to imagine living in 2020.

No conceivable redrawing of school districts or integration of individual classrooms will provide the range of immediate contacts to develop this extended social imagination and understanding. Development must necessarily depend upon vicarious experiences in which children see people through the eyes of the camera or the printed page. These experiences may be reinforced by contacts across class and racial lines but there is enough variety even in most suburban settings to allow children to practice their skills in intergroup and interpersonal communication. When suburban white students meet inner-city blacks for the first time they often make terrible blunders. They remain, however, remarkably optimistic that they can learn from their mistakes and return for another round of understanding.[15]

To summarize: school integration in the minds of its most vigorous upper and middle-class advocates is hardly a sufficient strategy for social understanding. It may not even appear to be a necessary one.

My version of American educational history may seem discouraging. Very few people really ever wanted common education—though they often had to settle for it. Very few people want to expose their children to a broad range of influences—unless they stem from more prestigious groups.

My intention is not discouragement. The total effect of a bit-by-bit response to educational inadequacy in this century has been an awesome increase in the production of schooling and the equalization of opportunity. Most apocalyptic accounts of the crisis in urban education appear in this historical perspective as simply the latest in a long series of highly effective goads to action.

The dynamics of this increase are, however, not particularly awe-inspiring: a response to inadequate training through marginal improvements rather than a cultural tension between democracy and inequality, yielding a release of opportunity. The major advantage, even from the most radical viewpoint, in reassessing the historical significance of ideas such as equality, is that the goals which then emerge as important may be talked about without shame and may be believed. While these goals do not ennoble discourse, they clarify communication. Appeals to an ideal such as equality, which may not be disclaimed but is not shared, break off discussion. Experimental programs which cannot be generalized breed suspicion. Professionals who act in one way but mythologize their behavior in another become strutters and puppets in the eyes of those they serve and liars to those they repress.

Serious consideration of the modest but real goals of American education also clarifies sources of stress which otherwise are falsely described as failures of will, or confrontations between ideals and reality. There is, for example, a persistent conflict between the desire to offer the working class an appropriate vocational education and the need to maintain enough common elements in all school curricula so that individuals may change their minds and their prospects. This conflict appeared early in this century in the first creation of vocational high schools. It reappeared again vehemently in the denunciations of James Conant's proposals for differentiated educational systems for slums and suburbs.[16] There is also a conflict, to choose another example, between the strategies for enlarging the pool of students eligible for élite institutions and for high-level professional roles. The largest group of reserve students not yet tapped is neither black nor poor, but middle-class, white, and female. Opening fuller access to this group involves almost no change in established patterns of educational behavior, tends characteristically to raise the standards of the training institutions, and does not require expensive individual subsidies. A black or poor-oriented admissions policy is, in contrast, changeful, standard-altering and costly. Unless equality is given both a purpose and a price, it is difficult to talk about these competing claimants upon scarce resources.

Taking seriously the goals to which people are actually committed has one final advantage. It describes the real rather than mythologized framework within which more radical goals and strategies will have to be developed. It is all very well to call for a revolution in American education. That call is but a pipe dream, however, unless it describes strategies which will work within established systems of constraints and will lead, in subsequent cycles of change, to enlarged possibilities. Such strategies should not upset the already delicate class and racial balance of large central cities and should offer attractive opportunities for cooperation to both Catholic and suburban school systems whose resistance would doom any program of class or racial integration.

A program which will satisfy these constraints must be designed to create a middle-class school for every child. I use the term *middle-*

class with a special twist to convey what the schools should be, rather than what they always are. Many middle-class children go to schools whose methods and behavioral patterns are inconsistent with the behavioral patterns they have learned and the opportunities they have sensed at home. These schools, rather than encouraging curiosity, repress it. Time is budgeted in little fixed units so that even with the most advanced and exciting curriculum students must learn to restrain their interest, turning their attention on and off as if they were themselves mechanical automatons. The organization of knowledge is treated as fixed rather than variable; its goals unspoken. This epistemology is the counterpart of an attitude towards social structures and institutions. Children are urged to work extremely hard towards unexamined ends.[17]

It would be foolish to argue that this blind education is inappropriate for all middle-class occupations and statuses. It is, however, clearly a mistake to train in this way men and women who will later enter either upper-level roles in public and private firms, the free professions, education, or science. This sense of economic rationality bolsters a larger feeling that training for passive dullness in which even excitement and commitment can be turned on or off is inhuman. The rebellion of middle-class students and parents against this inhumanity is a major force for change in American education.

The middle-class critique expresses itself in many ways: a fascination with the British infant school and with individualized modes of instruction, small, free high schools organized by school boards and underground newspapers hostile to the boards, creative writing classes, and student bills of rights. These programs potentially complement the black attack on discrimination and unequal achievement, so that a few radicals, educational critics, and professional schoolmen have been able to form a working alliance. A host of problems, however, beset the expansion and success of this alliance.

The most serious problem is a difference in educational imagery and teaching methods. The affluent critics of education characteristically describe themselves as advocates of freedom, spontaneity, individual fulfillment, and humanization. (A few, naively I believe, find the alliance attractive because they associate these qualities with blackness and poverty.) Most poor parents, eager for their children to succeed, imagine a system which stresses order, discipline, and concrete short-term achievement. Though they desire sympathy, warmth, and competence in individual teachers, the model of instruction they imagine for their schools is precisely the one to which the liberal critics object.[18]

Underlying these divergent images, on each side, are major misapprehensions. Liberal critics of educational authoritarianism describe their goals in terms of individual humanity. This always has the effect of denigrating the humanity of both their enemies and their somewhat suspicious friends, and impeding free communication. It also obscures the fact that teaching methods which develop curiosity, a critical perspective on established modes of analysis and behavior, and a passion for knowledge are the most appropriate training instruments for mobility and social and economic leadership. Poor parents have no way of intuitively understanding this and nothing in the talk of the affluent critics so far would let them into the dirty materialistic secret that liberal teaching methods pay off.

Aspiring low-income parents also suffer from a misapprehension. The design of the school of their dreams is, by and large, the design of the school in front of them. Order, discipline, achievement, and conformity are the ideals of the school, proclaimed even in the midst of the deluge. This convergence of desire and reality explains why, in many poor areas, there is an enormous fund of satisfaction with the schools. Teachers whose classroom strategies set the hair of liberal critics on end are locally admired.

There has been a good deal of criticism recently of the cultural distance between the school and the street. The shoe, I think, belongs on the other foot. Most schools in poor areas of our large cities are continuous with the culture of their areas.[19] Where the schools are successful in their own terms, they manage to cower their clients, by insisting on the authority relationship and making it stick with a delicate balance of prizes and punishments. For the most part, however, since the students, unlike factory workers, do not receive immediate rewards for their conformity, they rebel. The demands for obedience grow shrill as the students age, with less and less effect on their immediate behavior but more and more impact on the array of opportunities open to them. The teacher who feels she cannot control her students in the classroom in this way exercises enormous influence in confirming their class position and norms. They learn that knowledge is not for them, that they are potentially rowdy and that there are rules to the game of control.

Increasing the competence or sympathy of teachers within the ordinary instructional framework may help some students. A pattern in which knowledge is treated as a fixed set of tasks whose legitimacy, pace, and intensity are externally determined cannot, however, mobilize large numbers of lower-class children for expanded opportunities, because it confirms their subordinate position. Any educational program for equalization has to break the patterns of subordination and the social groupings and norms which make students feel subordinate. It may do this wisely by trying to engage and shift existing relationships rather than attacking them, but it is the gravest hypocrisy to pretend that the pursuit of equality will confirm rather than challenge the values of the poor.

FIVE

INTEGRATED
EDUCATION: *Possibilities*

The first element in an attack on the expectations and adaptive behavior of the lower class is to build an educational system in which both parents and children feel a sense of control and shared purpose. The controlling behavior has, however, to be directed towards opening external options rather than foreclosing them. Control which simply legitimates impotence is of little use to anyone except conservative defenders of the status quo.

The significance of the extension of control has been widely recognized and thoroughly distorted as it has entered into political discussions. In New York City, particularly, a shift in control portrayed as a "reconnection for learning," has led to a division of the city into subdistricts, each with a local school board. It is hazardous to predict the outcome of the change. I strongly suspect, however, that decentralization in New York and elsewhere is an inappropriate response to a correctly if dimly perceived problem.

The explicit purpose of decentralization is to increase the responsiveness and accountability of the schools to local geographic communities and, thereby, to enhance their legitimacy and effectiveness. The first requirement for responsiveness and accountability is vastly increased public understanding of the educational process. Control without understanding is quickly discovered as a shadow play. A parent may hold a teacher accountable for his performance, demanding to know why Johnny can't read. The limits of this demand are defined by the boundary between the elements in the learning situation which the teacher may vary and those over which he has no control. At each successive level of the educational hierarchy, new boundaries are defined and the accountable elements reordered. While a formal chart may attribute constantly expanding options to the men at the top of the hierarchy, the internal dynamics of a complex system give teachers options which are closed to even the most authoritarian school board. Holding a board responsible for every teacher would be as foolish as the alternative tactic of holding a teacher responsible for the policies of a board.

The shareholder's image of accountability in a large corporation, or even the citizen's image of legislative accountability, is inappropriate for interaction with the school system. A shareholder is properly satisfied if he can hold the directors of the corporation responsible for their performance. He need not be concerned with every engineer and manual laborer on the production line. Parents, in contrast, must focus their primary attention on a line official, the teacher, and therefore must share the director's or manager's knowledge of complex interactions within the entire system in which the line official's behavior is embedded.

This knowledge cannot be conveyed once and for all, as if the boundaries of roles and the limits of accountability were fixed and the product of wisdom was a shopping list of what cannot be done. In a system in which experiment is possible, roles variable, and research and development a norm, parents' knowledge has to be adapted to the evaluation of change.

There is no system of action comparable to the education of children in which the rewards for understanding a complex system and the processes of change are so great. Education can, therefore, make a high-capacity communications network worth building and worth paying attention to. The regrouping of school boards and programs of local elections and community meetings, hardly, however, create a network of sufficient capacity to develop the requisite understanding.

The only medium which reaches into individual homes with potentially adequate capacities of range, syntactical complexity, and volume is television. There are three major limitations on the current development of this potential:

- channel time is a scarce resource and hence dominated by a few centralized production centers and values.
- the pace and scheduling of programming is not adapted to the individual requirements of viewers.
- there are only indirect links between viewers and producers, so that the system is poorly integrated internally.

A desire for a "reconnection for learning," might be a major goad to the construction of new television systems which would reduce these limitations through:

- the increase in the number of channels and hence the increase in the number of specialized program sources.
- the repetition of programs to serve varied schedules and the increased tolerance for discursive communication.
- the linkage of communication components including libraries, home to studio feedback mechanisms, and local studios where viewers can turn into producers.

Improving the practice of accountability is not likely to excite anyone enough to bear the heavy costs of planning and building a new communications system. Nor should it. New television systems can penetrate directly into the instructional tasks and problems of shaping middle-class environments. These direct uses should define the major outlines of new systems of communication and justify their costs.

For the school to dominate its local culture, rather than succumbing, it has to expand its domain. The walls of buildings are, however, not easily stretched. Students come for a few hours and then leave. Children enter but their parents stay behind.

Television breaks down walls. Child development experts can talk with parents of infants or would-be parents. Adults can learn new work skills and children can come to see that school and its protocols are not solely designed for them. Parents and children can share in learning with and from one another in joint courses without leaving their homes.

Television also alters the balance of control between student and teacher. It allows viewers to pay sustained attention without distracting influences and, if they wish, to be inattentive without the embarrassment which inhibits tuning in again. Paradoxically, as the viewer gains control, the credibility of the instructor (Walt Disney or the ETV lecturer) is increased.[2]

There are two extreme views of the potential relationship between expanded television instruction and the design of total school systems. On one side, a few grand theorists imagine that children will spend most of their instructional time in front of home television sets and computer consoles and will come to school to meet their friends and to learn the techniques of group problem solving.[3] At the other extreme, many people can simply imagine an extension of the present patterns in which schools have integrated a limited amount of televised instruction into their ordinary procedures and treat the commercial networks as benevolent thieves, stealing children's time but occasionally leaving presents in return.

Neither extreme is either exciting or compelling. While it will be possible in a very short period to provide parents and children at home with a broad range of instructional services, it's highly unlikely that the major burden of teaching will be borne by video instructors. There is too much richness of response in a teacher-student relationship to be accommodated principally by a remote interaction. A child may, for example, make a mistake in answering a question for a great many different reasons. One of the most common reasons is that he is answering correctly his personal interpretation of the meaning of the question. Only sensitive interrogation, of the sort which usually defies automation, can discern his understanding of the question and the credibility of his answer.

Teachers play an important role even when children are working individually at a body of materials which may include both books and films. Only adults who know and care can answer on-the-spot a series of difficult questions. When the child is doing one thing well, should he always push on or should his attention sometimes be turned to another area of potential interest? If turned, why and with what participation on the child's part? [4]

When a choice has to be made between a system which insures very rapid but very narrow response and one which is slower, more uncertain, and richer, educational technologists may wisely choose the old method done well. The present conservative response to the use of television in the schools is not, however, a fair measure of the impact of systems with much broader capacities. Even skilled teachers working in small settings with a few children are often forced to waste the opportunities which intimacy provides. They must, as part of the appropriate instructional process, lay out the details of a well-structured idea whose outlines the students already understand. They must, similarly, often talk beyond their competence or spin images with words which might better be conveyed with pictures.[5]

The research evidence is unambiguous. Television and computer-assisted instruction can carry lectures, allow students to practice detailed competencies, and build images as well or often better than an immediate teacher. The research, however, does not test the relevance of the item-by-item, media-by-media findings to whole instructional systems. Presumably, it is both sensible and efficient for teachers to cherish the settings of intimacy rather than wasting them on drill-and-practice or lectures. These tasks can be performed effectively for large numbers of students linked in remote television and computer networks.

The presumption is, unfortunately, problematic. A remote network, to work effectively, must be as accessible as the teacher's own capability to switch gears. An individual instructor may be gently questioning one moment and then turn around and begin a lecture;

he may explain an idea one period and administer a diagnostic test the next. The opportunity he wastes by, for example, lecturing to a small group (perhaps in a field he does not know very well) is compensated by his ease of switching, his flexibility in planning, and his confidence that mechanical failures will not intrude.

The idea that it is useful to divide the instructional process into stages and to develop appropriate communication strategies for each is an untested dream. Experiments on particular components and successful programs here and there across the country increase the credibility of the dream but cannot fully support it. It's important, nevertheless, to explicate the dream. Only the image of a complete system explains why so many valuable components are unused. Many classrooms are supplied with television sets; many schools with closed-circuit systems. Without the linkages which would integrate them flexibly into the instructional process, the sets remain dark and the systems are consigned to humdrum trivia.

More significantly, the technological dream suggests that it is possible to alter the boundaries of educational systems and change the distribution of information without threatening powerful interests. It suggests that it might be possible to change the design of schools and school systems without serious threat.

The previous chapter began with the problem of integrating big-city school systems. The most prestigious integration plan is the creation of giant educational parks, serving large heterogeneous populations, hopefully to include both city residents and suburbanites. These parks would be composed of a full range of facilities, serving students of every age. Individual units within the park might be small, but they would share a common set of expensive libraries, auditoriums, laboratories and gymnasia, and specialized personnel.

The most serious problem of the park plan is that it challenges almost everyone's preferences in return for its benefits. Most children would find their travel time to school increased. The already intense conflicts over converting large tracts of land from one use to another would be exacerbated. Despite every attempt to build intimacy into the mammoth setting, most people will suspect that bigness will out and that the park will be a microcosm of a crowded central business district. Indeed, in its attempt to create a bounded campus which reproduces the variety of the city itself, the park plan is linked in its imagery and values to a classic conception of the dense and cosmopolitan central city.

The educational park is most appropriate as a rational building plan for small cities and the fringes of large metropolitan areas. It would make very good sense, for example, for state governments to build comprehensive educational facilities in advance of settlement. This would reduce the force of the complaint in many new suburbs that the press of school taxes is so great that they can't afford to make room for the prolific poor. Advance construction would make it considerably easier to introduce low-income families into planned developments.

Within built-up areas, an integrated school plan must be more respectful of the established forms of the city. In a large metropolis connected by elaborate transportation and communications lines, it is a form of radical nostalgia to imagine that a common campus will bring people together. An educational design should exploit and extend the established lines of connection, rather than going back to an inadequate model of the past.

Design, as I said in the very first paragraph of this book, is a detailed and sweaty job. What follows is only a sketch outline of the parts of a school system for a large American city. The sketch cannot possibly answer all the appropriate questions about costs, benefits, and implementation. It is intended in its rough form to serve three purposes:

- to give concrete meaning to the abstract idea that it is important to consider the internal integration of all the components of a communications network, rather than simply the capacity of one component or another.

- to suggest that there are approaches to integration and equalization which have hardly been broached in the standard discussions of urban education.

- to emphsize, by contrast, the limitations of attempts to alter communication patterns by changing the lines of formal authority.

This last purpose provides the connection to systems other than education and to the largest political framework in which new communication networks may be set.

I imagine a school system organized around six spatially defined units connected by a network of wires, buses, and postal delivery trucks. Each of the units and the network are familiar to most educators. My proposal is simply that those elements that have been tried, one by one, here and there, be pulled together into an integrated system and addressed to the educational dilemmas of the largest cities in the nation.

My proposal is also consistent with innovative proposals which are more challenging to school norms or modes of finance. It describes the small, stable settings which make it possible to sustain open classrooms and free, responsive teaching by adults who are able to care about children because they know them.[6] It similarly describes a way of providing instructional support, guidance, and supervision for a variety of public and private schools. This should make it possible to allow parents to choose schools freely and wisely and to experiment with new forms of payment.[7]

The proposal is intended for experimentation in districts within cities but it can be generalized. The only critical specification for the experiment is that it must test the complex system not its separate components. Most educational engineering suffers unfortunately from fragmented implementation and the consequent distressing evaluative report of "no significant difference."

The six spatial elements are:

> homes
> widely scattered study centers
> small local schools
> specialized schools
> central management and instructional libraries and studios
> specialized recreational centers

The connecting network would provide a small amount of channel space and feedback capacity to homes; broader capacities to study centers, local, and specialized schools.

The key to the proposal is the small, and stable, local school. Within the experimental district, new schools should be built to house only two or three classes at each grade level; old schools broken up into genuinely separate units. These little schools would be stable because children would no longer be forced to change as their parents moved from home to home within the same general area. Children should remain in their groups so long as their families lived within very large catchment zones. School stability is a more important value than accessibility and minimal travel time.

These small schools would not yield interclass or interracial integration. They might, however, provide a setting in which parents, teachers, and children could come to know one another and adapt their behavior to this knowledge. The simple shortage of manpower would press students into active roles in the organization of the school. The big school, almost by its very design, teaches lower-class children to assume a specialized lower-class role. Multiplying the opportunities for participation in an outward directed institution is an essential step in the attack on this role.[8]

Small schools must be connected if they are to integrate rather than fragment the city. The complement of stable smallness is a system of specialized learning centers in which children from many parts of the city would be grouped together to work on topics which they had shared in both choosing and shaping and which they could pursue with sustained attention. These centers could be of two types. The first would bring students together who shared a common interest, such as astronomy or creative writing, or were ready for a specialized program as part of their ordinary educational progress. The second type would be designed to exploit the variety of student backgrounds whatever the initial interests. Imagine, for example, a studio which allowed fifth graders from across the city to work for a month planning an ideal city.

These centers, like the educational park, would impose new travel costs on most students. Unlike the park scheme, the inconvenience would extend for only a month or two at a time and be mitigated, at least in part, by the closeness of the home environment.

New communications and information technologies complement this scheme for the reorganization of spatial units and the movement of pupils. The most important reason for housing children throughout the school year in the same building and dividing their day, as they grow older, into short uniform periods is to solve a complex management problem. Multiple buildings, changeable schedules, and irregular time units present almost insuperable obstacles to the pencil and paper schedule clerk. While public attention is usually focused on the potential of computers for instruction, professionals have been applying them to scheduling and other management tasks. What they have not fully realized, however, are the possible directions in the path they have already trod. Without challenging accepted roles, districts could accelerate the development of computer management systems to break the grip of restricted spatial and temporal scheduling. Teachers and students can be deployed, buses rerouted, and records kept without marshalling the troops under a single roof.[9]

When remote communication technologies are applied to the instructional tasks themselves, the possibility of many roofs increases. It would be easy, once students had returned to their base school from two months at a specialized center, to continue their contacts with each other through occasional meetings. It would also be possible to supply them with books and pamphlets for independent study or correspondence courses.

Beyond these strategies, which rely heavily on printed materials, districts should supply remote video and computer instruction. A few courses might reach into homes but it probably won't be feasible to provide the number of channels necessary for a complete instructional program in everyone's living room. Scattered study centers in apartments, store-fronts, or row homes, could, however, be equipped with adequate capacities. The study centers would be principally used after school hours as quiet oases outside the home. They might, however, also serve some students as convenient links into the remote network during the day.

Schools themselves would, of course, have higher capacities still, with more integrating links: libraries as extended memories, teachers as processing aids.

The wired school system would reduce the rigidity which has inhibited the current use of televised instruction. Any single broadcast is appropriate for use, now, by only a small percentage of teachers. And yet, of course, now is the only time for viewing. Ordering film material from a central library is comparably clumsy. The films are rarely sequential, often late, and must be requested far in advance. As a result, they are either not used or used badly. This reduces the demand for film products and, in sequence, their supply, their credibility, their worth, and back again to the demand.

Cheap video recorders and wired systems may break this cycle. Teachers can request video tapes during the day for nighttime transmission from the central library. The recorded selection would be available the next morning, though the master would remain at the central location. The reproduction could be erased if the cost of tape and storage were greater than those of transmission. Commercial broadcasts could be similarly copied for use at appropriate times.

The hardest materials to share across space are books. It is already possible to build standard reference collections in every school through micro-recording but no new technology replaces the individual book for general use: take it home, put it in your pocket, scan it on the train, read it in the bathtub. Any school system worthy of the name will have to provide great numbers of books at every location.

There is a chic myth which denies this necessity and heralds the beginning of the postliterate age. Nonsense. Postliteracy is a mirage which vanishes as the student pushes deeper and deeper. There is no reason for thinking of visual and oral media as anything but complementary to the range and depth of print.

Quite apart from its impact on particular modes of instruction, a wired school system would extend the general capacity for innovation. In most schools in this country, there is no one whose major responsibility is to sort and transmit new ideas, encourage teachers to innovate in their practice, and to share their experiences with others.[10] The burden of scanning the research literature and testing new ideas is cast upon the teacher. The supervisory staff may help but its attention is ordinarily directed to more pressing though not necessarily more important problems of conventional practice. Moreover, the role of the principal as guide to new techniques is inevitably corrupted by his simultaneous role as supervisor and evaluator. Some principals manage this tension quite successfully, but for most there is an intractable conflict between the two tasks.

There is no way of changing behavior while avoiding this conflict entirely. Special summer or year-long institutes have been set up to train educators in new curricula or teaching methods. These programs have succeeded when the teachers, back in their own schools, received the interested support of their colleagues and supervisors. The programs have failed where the insecure innovators were returned to hostile environments.

A wired school system might reduce the tensions generated by innovative training by increasing the general accessibility of new ideas. At the central station, teams of teachers and researchers could develop libraries of successful curricular units or lessons, evaluations of teaching strategies and tactics, and guides to substantive fields of knowledge and instructional materials. Without wire, quick mail or delivery service could retrieve an item in a few days. Remote access through a wired system could, however, allow teachers to scan alternatives before choosing a particular item and to poke under odd categories which might house items of interest.

This central library should not be conceptually remote from the field teachers. They could enter their experiences into the library. If accepted as producers of knowledge, I suspect they would become much more open-minded and experimental consumers. Networks of innovative teachers, coming to know one another through their library publications could help one another by phone or in person. This help would be particularly useful for teachers who found themselves in local school settings in which the norm was defeat, in which everyone said that nothing new or nothing good could be done.[11]

The library for teachers would also be welcomed by central curriculum designers already within the school systems. With a complementary television capacity, the wired library would spread new ideas into scattered classrooms and make it easier for curriculum designers to estimate the difficulties encountered by teachers. The school system, with increased communication capacities, could be centrally controlled and yet provide participation and response. The usual polarity between decentralized participation and central authority is a deception. In New York City, school leaders are already discovering that they must increase their central competence to serve the goals of the decentralized system.

Access to an educational library should not be confined to professional schoolmen. The index and items themselves might be written for laymen—including parents. The accessibility of the library may involve teachers in more troubles than they would ordinarily choose. You may imagine the annoyance of a Bronx teacher confronted by a parent with an insistent demand: "Why aren't *you* using that great unit developed in California and successfully employed by two Queens teachers?" All in all, however, the badgering would be preferable to either the shrill but impotent call for quality or the passive but disengaged deference to authority. If professional and public images are to converge, then professionals will have to be ready to talk honestly and expertly with their clients.

This description of the wired school system quite deliberately does not circle back to tie together the instructional network with the politics of school decentralization and accountability. The nature of that tie depends upon a general conception of the relationship between institutional design and the flow of information. That conception is the subject of the next chapter.

SIX

COMMUNICATION
AND BARBARISM

The ideal of reaching out across boundaries of class, race, ethnicity, and space to share images and values is a very old dream. In a variety of settings it has provided the noblest expression of the desire for understanding and cooperative humanity. This nobility is not demeaned in the least by acknowledging the selfish bases of the desire for extended contact. Not even in churches are men really expected to be pure of heart before they enter into communion. People begin to talk because they hope to be persuasive; they listen because they want to be heard. The harmony they seek through mutual understanding is the achievement of a desired order of values and relationships.

I emphasize the universality of this selfishness so as not to seem to be peculiarly harsh upon one of its special manifestations. The most general impulse behind efforts at intergroup communication in American cities has been the fear of substantial burghers that the lower classes were cultural barbarians and, therefore, threats to peace and tranquility. *Barbarian* is a harsh characterization—and rather old fashioned now in its usage—but many blacks (and many young people) will recognize it as the essential rhetoric of the perspective they resent. At other times, it has been equally resented by both "honest workingmen" and by nouveau riche, suffering from the scorn of their "betters."

There is ample reason for resentment. Fear and ignorance are frequently compounded to produce a picture of the barbarian who is not simply outside the culture but is uncultured, and is thereby less than a civil man. Nevertheless, behind the charge of barbarism has always been an essentially correct élite perception that those who are not known by their presumptive leaders cannot be adequately governed. Elites have also often presumed that those whom they do not know, do not know them. This mistaken presumption has brought grief to many political careers.

It may seem strange, particularly from the perspective of the university, to single out the threat of lower-class barbarism as an impulse to communication. The current hue and cry is the barbarism of youth. In the minds of their advocates, the barbarians are creative, imaginative, wise, and vigorous; in their detractors', irresponsible and immoral. Both images are curiously alike in substance, differing only in their evaluation. Both also are very old. Whenever adults are deeply involved in changing their own values and behavior, they find the socialization of the young peculiarly difficult. Imagining that its social dilemmas are problems of youth, the adult world distracts attention from more serious sources of internal conflict.

Young people are mobile, yet clustered together in institutions which allow them to be organized; they are both coerced consumers of knowledge and have unique access to a forum which allows them to express their reactions to ideas. There is, however, neither a unique wisdom nor foresight in youth. Choose any one of a number of pressing issues: the war in Indo-China, the natural ecology of man, the distribution of income, or the revision of personal and collective priorities. The decisive critical attack in each one of these problem areas has come from experts whose maturity and knowledge are unimpeachable. Indeed, the men who make policy commonly feel put down as somehow less sophisticated and knowledgeable than their adult critics. Loading the burden of dissent onto the young and transforming issues into a conflict of generations conveniently allays this inferiority. It has been much easier for example to deal with student dissent and to learn to listen to young people than to accommodate to the harsher fact that most knowledgeable men found American policy in Indo-China rooted in misconceptions and deliberate lies.

The apprehension of lower-class, rather than youthful, barbarism is an honest confrontation of an intrinsic problem in social hierarchies. The problem, quite simply is, Will the people at the bottom of the hierarchy, enjoying relatively limited power and rewards, accept the goals of their superiors sufficiently to work capably and live virtuously?

This problem appears repeatedly as the impetus to social communication. Public schools were begun to civilize the barbarians, police corps to tame them, personnel departments in factories to engage their loyalties. Almost always, however, communication intended only for control has proven richer than its designers imagined. Projected listeners turn into speakers: men who mean only to influence others are themselves altered in the process.

This experience of the past is likely to be repeated in the future. I find it impossible to imagine any new communications network which does not build, with tension, a two-way street. The proposal for a wired school system illustrates the tension. On the one side, the barbarians are suffused with the culture of the middle class; on the other, they enjoy so far unimagined possibilities for influence and active participation. The search for pure networks, either linking unselfishly or only in one direction is hopeless, and the rhetoric of purity can bedevil every design effort. The appropriate answer to the taunt, "You're just talking to us in order to control us!" is, "Of course. Now let's talk about how we are going to talk."

Elite attempts to control the barbarians have taken many forms. The dangerous classes have been simultaneously propagandized and coerced; paid off with welfare and tempted with democratic rights; manipulated at school and work and rewarded with opportunity and riches. In the late nineteenth century, all of these forms of control operated in the same local environment and impinged upon one another. School teachers, factory managers and ward bosses, policemen and settlement house residents, editors and charity agents—whether as ally or as enemy—saw each other as participants in a general struggle to define the norms of both individual and community life.[1]

Times have changed. Each of the forms of control has developed in its own way. The spatial separation of home and jobs, and the diversity of employment in large cities, have particularly isolated the world of work. While relations in store, office, and factory are the major determinants of status and power, they are difficult to discuss publicly or to introduce into realistic political debate. The managers of business firms, perhaps from the beginning of time and certainly since the nineteenth century, have realized that their apprehensions of barbarism and those of state officials were connected. The good worker meshed with the good citizen; obedience and responsiveness on the job with social harmony and a respect for law and order on the street.

Through most of the nineteenth and early twentieth century, this mesh was a prime concern of businessmen. In recent years, however, the concern has been reduced or curiously imbalanced. When, for example, businessmen and economists join together to plan for the future they usually emphasize the social programs and investments which will produce the skills and manpower needed for tomorrow's industry. Changes in the organization of work are givens, to which the rest of society must adapt. Rarely do they inquire into the forms of social relations on the job which might produce a desirable citizen. It seems old-fashioned, now that unions have been legalized, to continue to repeat the old radical pleas for democracy at work.

The other forms of control, as distinct as they may have become, have not enjoyed—or suffered—the same degree of isolation as the world of work. Indeed, we are now caught up in one of those periodic moments when reconnection rather than further separation is a pressing item on the urban public agenda. Underlying all of the talk and the shouting about decentralization, neighborhood control, citizen participation, and the new politics, is the search for a new synthesis of institutions and relationships. For the most part, the goal of reconnection is phrased as a counterattack on élite influences. In fact, the counterattack so far has succeeded only where it promises to extend élite security rather than to imperil it. Community control in inner-city neighborhoods is fine as long as it leaves the suburbs in command of their own resources.

If those concerned with counterattack and reconnection are to succeed at all in satisfying their own goals they will have to remember and respect the pressures which altered the pattern of nineteenth-century community life. It would be foolish to go back to the personal, arbitrary, and impotent ward politics of 1870. The cruelest future would be a mindless recapitulation of the past.[2]

Two complementary processes altered the institutional forms of the control of barbarism. The first was a movement to centralize authority and to regularize bureaucratic procedures and the recruitment of personnel. Even the most skilled autocrat could not hope to supervise thousands of workers and to recruit hundreds of new recruits annually without a set of bureaucratic standards and a measure of professionalization. Dominated as they often were by businessmen, city governments adopted—though always with a difference—the norms of the large modern corporation. The second process was the separation of the bureaucracies from one another. This separation was the professional counterpart of the earlier division of turfs. Once ward leaders had been warned to stay in their own territories, now police chiefs were cautioned to keep their noses out of the schools; social workers were excluded from party politics.

The detailed processes of bureaucratization, centralization, and separation varied in each city and within different institutional settings. I am interested here only in general patterns and have chosen illustrations which are strategically important but not unique. The general point of these illustrations is an extension of what I have already said about schools: reconnection cannot solely or even principally proceed through a return to localism or a spatial realignment of people and facilities.

Organized full-time police forces have been the major instruments of civil control for more than a hundred years in large American cities. The linkage between "criminal" and "lower" classes was very explicit in the initial formation of police forces.[3] While the rhetoric has softened through time and the instrument is sometimes turned against its designers, the control function is only lightly hidden under the surface of activity.

Through most of the last century, efforts to improve this control function have focused around three great tasks:

- increasing the effectiveness and legitimacy of the performance of the individual and largely isolated officer.
- reducing the imperium of district captains and rendering them accountable to their superiors.
- developing capacities for deploying resources flexibly and responsively across large urban spaces.

There have been two usual methods of approaching these tasks. The first has been to raise the level of training required for entrance into police forces and promotion within them. The second has been the expansion of the internal communications system. This expansion has depended both upon organizational realignment and heavy investments in advanced technologies. In successive stages, the nation's police forces have led all other agencies in the use of the telegraph, telephone, fixed point and mobile radio, closed circuit television, remote detection, and computerized information management.

It is always possible to quarrel about the impact of this or that technological or organizational change. Police forces, as other bureaucracies, have a remarkable ability to assimilate innovations without altering their behavior. In the long perspective of the century, however, expanded training and internal communications have been successful. Police performance on a broad range of dimensions has been improved and central control enhanced.

This shift in the locus of police power ramifies through the whole political structure. Though the real adaptability of forces to special neighborhood conditions may have been improved, the planning of adaptation has shifted to the center and been separated from local constituencies. District politicians may still march into station houses; district captains may even form local citizens councils, but major decisions are made at headquarters. The power of the center is, of course, not absolute. As in any complex bureaucracy, the preferences of the lowliest officials, particularly if they are organized, constrain the options of the central directors. Nevertheless, it is fair to describe the police commissioners of the 1970s as the beneficiaries of a long managerial revolution.[4]

The reality of central power makes police forces amenable to large-scale influences. The federal government, with funds to finance new technologies or to constrain unconstitutional tactics, now has the ability to alter police behavior. Mayors or review boards may fairly hold commissioners accountable for the design and performance of their organizations.

The very reality of their power reinforces the self-protective impulses of the central professionals. From the 1870s on, a long string of famous investigations of urban police forces has been directed towards reducing corruption and the influence of party politics and accelerating the rise in standards of entrance and promotion. While this vein of inquiry is not entirely exhausted, it has been complemented by critical studies of the basic organization of police services and the accountability of officials. These new emphases are much more threatening to professionals than the older stress on training, virtue, and independence. What is now open for discussion is the general design of systems of social control.

The police experience is not unique. In virtually every public service system, remote communications and central control generate a sharp increase in the internal documentation of performance. A police chief wants to know where his cars are located and he must develop explicit criteria for computerized deployment. A school superintendent has similiar information needs. Where are his teachers? What are they doing? What are the criteria for assignment? What deployment of resources changes the output of the schools? In other areas, national planners have gone beyond their fifty-year old interest in indicators of economic performance and now cultivate a broad range of social measures. Legislators, despairing of the maze of their own making, are encouraging computerized tracing of the progress of bills, reducing the power of the few experienced hands who had mastered the intricacies of the legislative system. Welfare bureaucracies have become so large that reasonable management, quite apart from external pressure, demands that the informal rules caseworkers use to control clients must be observed and analyzed.[5]

The increase in the internal documentation of performance opens remarkable opportunities for systems engineering and invention. It also moves towards more open bureaucracies, capable of being known rather than closed to inspecting eyes. Any program to expand public understanding or to alter the balance of power between groups must build upon this potential. Popular assumptions that government is becoming less knowable and requires simplification distract attention from the most radical possibilities. The mistaken assumption stems from a confusion between familiarity and understanding. A local police captain or school teacher may be an old friend, he may be accessible, he may belong to the dominant group in the neighborhood, and yet, despite all those qualities, may be unable to convey a sense of what makes the schools or the police tick. Indeed, his favors and his individual efforts—precious as they are—may only disguise his impotence before the larger pressures which he does not understand or cannot control.

It is difficult to grasp the opportunities in open bureaucracies without a communications network capable of linking professionals with their clients and publics. Attempts to build such networks immediately confront the separation of bureaucracies from one another. The police, in order to accomplish their own internal transformation, have striven to detach themselves from the influences of neighborhood politicians. Schoolmen have done the same. To solve the nagging problems of 1900, they have created a bounded world of their own choosing. Insofar as the schools needed clinical or therapeutic professionals, they developed them within the walls. Insofar as they needed ties to local parents, they built them within a specialized framework acceptable to their own norms rather than politicizing education. P.T.A.s—yes; neighborhood councils—no.

There is a host of dimensions which distinguish the history of educational from police systems. The management of learning was very difficult to centralize and so a wide range of initiatives was left to field officers. Ironically, this narrowed the elements of central control and made them appear peculiarly restrictive. Teachers sensed that they were more regulated than guided. In the struggle against restrictive limits, images of decentralization have been deployed as weapons of attack. In fact, however, the development of a broad range of new curricula and teaching formats, responsive to a varied student body, has everywhere generated an enormous growth in centralized professional staffs, both within school systems and in research institutes, business firms, and universities. Where school systems fail to develop or use this professional capacity, decentralization becomes a formula for the preservation of traditional practice.

The differences between the police and the schools have not eliminated the overall similarity in their histories. While many functions were brought within the boundaries of the schools, school people generally isolated themselves from issues of the police, safety and welfare, community development, the organization of health services, land use, the design of social communication, and the framework of politics. Separation to enhance internal control necessarily reduced their external influence on their own fate.

This separation necessarily plagues every attempt to understand and change the individual bureaucracies. The schools and the police can no more be comprehended in isolation than they can be separately reformed. We are now in a period of institutional invention. Here and there across the country, community clinics have, for example, tried to reach out to their constituents rather than waiting for them to enter the marble palace. Always, the outreach teams find themselves messengers of more than health. Babysitting, landlord problems, school issues, police relations—all seem to fall within their purview and to strain budgets meant only to fund health services.[6]

Established institutions of public communication have felt this strain for several generations, and have adapted to it. These adaptations in many cases—notably in agencies concerned with adult education and community organization—have come to reflect the restrictive effect of the separation of individual bureaucracies.

The organizational history of adult education in the first half of this century has been influenced by the larger struggle between trainers and educators. On the one side, some theorists and practitioners, with very substantial support from large foundations, cast adult institutions in the mold of the liberal arts college. On the other side, a much larger group went about the business of training immigrants to be Americans, up-dating the skills of accountants, introducing housewives to the joys of bridge, and reinforcing the faith of worried parishioners.

While differences remain, the sounds of battle have been muted. The creation of the Adult Education Association as a unified national organization in the 1950s was accompanied by a recognition of the common foundation of virtually all adult educational activities: the learners come voluntarily in response to a self-perceived need. All adult instructional planning, whether the subject is Socrates, gourmet cooking, or international politics, must revolve around the facts of voluntarism and need. These facts develop opportunities largely denied to schools for children which depend heavily upon both coercion and the external definition of necessary learning. Exploiting these opportunities adult educators are quite properly prideful of their pedagogical inventiveness and their relevance. Unlike professionals in most other institutional areas they have also paid attention to national communications policy. In the nineteen twenties and thirties, they fought for radio frequencies; in the fifties for television channels. Today, they are uniquely conscious of the importance of cable television and wired cities.[7]

Despite this history and these sensitivities, adult educators have not been able to project themselves into the center of the community development effort. Voluntarism and need, as broad as they are, have somehow been too fragile a bridge to all of the potential clients. The largest study of the educational activities of adults found, in the early sixties, that one adult in five had been involved in some sort of instructional program in the previous year, more than half since leaving school. This enormous body of students was, however, heavily concentrated in upper income and educational groups. Those who had already succeeded at school and at work came to do more.[8]

This class distribution reveals the limits of voluntarism and need. Self-perceptions of need are almost always connected to some potential for action. Asking people to know, or creating a situation in which they need knowledge, is part of the same act as creating a system of action which rewards information. (Earlier, I described these rewards as external integration.) Men need vocational training where it may yield a job. They need to learn skills of self-reporting and historical statement where the ability to fill out a medical form will generate therapy in return.

The institutions of adult education have prospered where they are directly attached to existing structures of opportunity and perceptions of need. In business firms and government agencies, adult training courses help men get ahead. Even the Great Books program appears to provide a ticket into a socially esteemed world of discourse. The professionals have rarely, however, projected themselves into the restructuring of opportunities or the recombination of functions. Detached from the world of active research and speculation, they have depended upon purveying established truths and well-known skills. First, labor unions as direct action agencies and, now, community development corporations, residents groups, and health consortiums have been largely outside their domain. As a result of their success in the established pattern, adult educators have never been able to develop an image of themselves as vitally concerned with change, nor to share their own perceptions of the social significance of communications policy.

The effect of the separation of institutions of class interaction is felt deeply not only by adult educators but by the social workers who staff settlement houses, community centers, neighborhood, and social service organizations. The history of their institutions and their own personal perspectives often express the separation more than oppose it. Even radical community organizers who criticize the social work establishment bitterly often founder on the rocks of a differentiated world. Locally, they may talk about everything. As they seek to influence city-wide behavior, they become functional specialists building a coalition around the schools, or the police, or a highway program. The synthetic local vision is attenuated.

Both staid social workers and radical community organizers would undoubtedly deny that their activities are associated with an élite attack on barbarism. The intellectual referents, particularly for those wishing to redistribute power to the neighborhoods, are the inherent territorial interests of all men, the brotherhood of neighbors, or the colonial counterattack against the imperialism of central business districts.[9]

I have no interest in contesting ideologies and identities. Each man

105

is free to choose his own roots. A decent respect for history, however, compels recognition of a simple fact: most of the institutions designed to organize the poor were externally designed to reach into the world of the poor and to stabilize it. The power of this reach downwards has been so great that it has assimilated and legitimated virtually all radical efforts to reach upwards. Unions, Panthers, and neighborhood councils—all are either tamed or die.[10]

The history of this intervention does not begin with citizen participation in the "War on Poverty" or the Model Cities program. From the first decades of the nineteenth century, middle-class groups in American cities, possessed by a fear of barbarism, have wrestled with the organizational task of tranquilizing the lower classes. Associations with duel goals of helping the poor materially and of providing direct middle-class models for them were formed in virtually every large city by the middle of the century. Characteristically, these associations were divided by their conflicting goals. They were, on the one hand, dedicated to assisting the poor with money, food, clothing, or other supplies. On the other hand, they wanted to train them to be strong, law-abiding, God-fearing, and independent souls. The language used to describe the conflict between dependence and independence may now seem curiously old-fashioned. The dilemma was, however, real enough and the amateur altruists remained locked in its grip so long as they preserved the two goals together.[11]

The only way out of the dilemma was to separate the goals and to pursue them independently. This, in fact is what happened. In a series of steps, the tasks of giving material assistance were sorted out. The latest moves towards a guaranteed annual income or negative income tax, though couched as criticism of the welfare bureaucracy, are the culmination of a long process by which income support has come to stand on its own ideological legs. To be entirely fair, the legs are still somewhat wobbly. The fear of creating a dependent generation still is expressed in public debate and professional dispensers of aid still wrestle with psychological models of dependence and guidance. There is, however, in many agencies a vigorous rejection of these worries. "What the poor lack," the new wisdom has it, "is money. Let's give them some!"

The concept of extending to the poor a direct model of middle-class life, wrapped up in the nineteenth century with the charitable enterprise, has gone its own partially independent way. Over the course of the nineteenth century, missionaries in a great many environments learned that they had to listen before they could speak; that they had to understand before they could intervene. In American cities, this realization was expressed in the development of settlement houses in which resident bourgeois came both to organize, assist, and comprehend the poor.

The separation between the provision of material support and the adaptive organization of community life as envisaged by the settlement workers has never been complete. Workers in each of the fields have shared some common professional affiliations, common tasks, and a common interest in telling society about the poor. This telling, sometimes described by historians of both the turn of the century and the 1960s as a "discovery of poverty," has served the important purpose of encouraging large publics to support the bridge functions of the professionals. Even the most direct initiatives of the poor in establishing their case before the world have been mediated through the eyes of the professionals. They attribute meaning to initiatives and link that meaning to responsive action. This mediation generates frustration when even so elemental an act as a riot is surrounded— almost suffocated—by studies, and enhances the interpreters more than the actors. There is no way, however, of communicating without a channel; of switching from one code to another without an interpreter.

The separation has, more importantly, never been complete because the two approaches are complementary. Despite the strains which generated their division, providers and organizers need one another to establish contacts between professionals, their clients and the policy issues which effect them. The providers, from the very beginning of the century, wrestled with the problem of coordinating their activities. The development of health and welfare councils as coordinating mechanisms left them, however, with a sense of detachment from their service constituencies. The councils, whatever their virtues, had professionals talking only to themselves or to their business supporters in the united community funds.

Even prior to World War II, small groups of social workers had tried to break out of this restrictive framework to link the idea of the comprehensive provision of services to a vaguely defined image of broad public participation in the process of welfare planning. They experimented with community health planning in Cincinnati from 1917–1920 and tried to formulate general principles at national conventions in 1939 and 1940. Challenged recently to demonstrate their concern, the activities of these pre-war groups have served social workers as evidence of hallowed professional interest.[12]

The constituency problem was not easily solved by social workers themselves. The papers on community organization presented to the National Conference on Social Welfare in 1958, at a distance of only a little more than a decade, seem quaint and old-fashioned. The speakers urged greater participation in welfare decisions. They meant that more agencies should join in council, not that the process should be broadly politicized. Local leaders, the speakers enjoined, would have to be recruited and trained by social workers so they could join the lay boards of agencies and coordinating councils.[13]

The vastly expanded demands for participation in the 1960s burst like an avalanche upon this highly professional effort to reach out to larger constituencies. It burst also upon those workers who had stayed close to their neighborhood bases, and had not followed cosmopolitan professionals into greener fields. The settlement houses of the early twentieth century had been influenced by an image of a small residential community providing a stable home in the midst of a changeful modern society. The city, as this image was translated into early academic sociology, was conceived as an aggregation of neighborhoods. Very quickly, however, even before its implications had been understood or tried, leaders of major settlement houses abandoned the image and moved outwards to find adequate bases for power and control over their environment. A ward, residents at Chicago's Hull House found, could not clean itself or protect its workers' industrial safety. The settlement leaders progressively focused their attention upon the city, and found it inadequate, and then the state —also wanting—and finally the national government.[14]

This movement upwards was a thoroughly reasonable pursuit of the appropriate scale at which groups could adapt to changeful conditions. Since, however, the expansion was not accompanied by an increased public capacity to operate at the larger scale, the leaders quickly isolated themselves from their old constituencies and institutions. Though they retained the symbols of the settlement house and integrated community development, the new allies who supported their efforts were found among the professional politicians and the leaders of organized labor.

The settlement houses were, meanwhile, left in the lurch. They continued to spread and they continued to provide local services, but they were almost wholly divorced from the images of community development and adaptation which had shaped their founding. Dependent upon conservative local united funds for support, they turned away from politics. Dependent upon professional social workers for leadership, they turned away from the explicit function of class integration they had adopted in the early days of resident amateurs. They ceased to be wholly, or even peculiarly, institutions characteristic of lower-income neighborhoods.

The result of these processes was not decay—indeed, the community center idea has prospered—but simply isolation. Faced with a new ideology of community control and a new array of institutional forms, the center organizers have pleaded that their experience and moral commitment be both acknowledged and respected.[15] Rarely, however, have they demonstrated their ability to broaden their own base of participation and to connect themselves with issues of public welfare policy. For the community center, as for the school, a pervasive localism and institutional separation, reduced both their external influence and their local impact. As long as national income distribution and housing policies are not local issues, then localism is a formula for impotence.

It would be easy to shrug off the limitations of social workers and adult educators and their occasional complaints of offended dignity. They are not responsible, after all, for the connection of local and general issues. They are not responsible for the allocations of funds between governmental services and the coordination of policy.

Those responsibilities fall squarely on the shoulders of the leaders of government. These leaders' current difficulties and discomfort cannot be dismissed. They now face what appears to them to be a disquieting attack on the legitimacy of representative institutions and the adequacy of the established modes of bureaucratic decision making. Threatened by the attack, they have the capability of defending themselves. Mayors, who perceived that their city-wide authority and responsibilities were diluted by Model Cities plans which sent funds directly to neighborhood groups, were able for example, to block the flow of money and alter program rules. The political leaders are not capable, however, of capturing the creative vigor in the attack and utilizing it for a complementary expansion of governmental initiative and popular participation. They are not capable because they lack an adequate communications network.

The scenario of the attack is virtually always the same. Choose any neighborhood in the United States which has been touched by the ethic of community participation. Describe the history of its Model Cities program, or its new public health clinic, community center, or manpower training effort. Planners or local activists try to energize residents around a particular expansion of opportunity. In order to capture attention and provide a channel for two-way interaction they set up a communications network of groups and meeting rooms, broadsides, and local publicity. Since a great many people only pay attention once action has begun, the initiators constantly find themselves doing more than the preceding level of assent would properly allow. Precisely as they begin to succeed, they are besieged with complaints that they really don't want participation or that the committee structure is not really representative of the grassroots—that is, of the latest group to pay attention and to feel that it needs to know what is going on.

The conflicts generated by the constantly expanding grassroots understandably confirms the defensive reaction of elected representatives. In several cases, they have even managed to cool the ardor of some early proponents of community control. They have not managed, however, to still the pervasive complaint that the structure of parties and representative institutions does not allow for adequate popular participation in the process of governance. Reform movements continue to argue that the voice of the people is not adequately heard in City Hall or party councils. Decentralization is still trumpeted as a way of reconnecting the citizen and his government. A new revisionist history has even been created. Old-style political machines are now viewed with some respect as having provided both expressive and functional participation to the lower classes. The bureaucratization of city agencies, the reduction of patronage, and the creation of councils elected from large or even city-wide districts have all eliminated a vital tie between classes and left the poor alienated and unrepresented.[16]

Each one of the elements in this complaint about participation and in this history may be countered. Reform in the name of the people is, after all, a very old American formulation. Indeed, many of the structural changes in cities which presumably have restricted participation were defended as instruments of democracy. The demand for community control in this view has ridden piggyback on a more abiding interest in black power. As soon as blacks expand their influence in central institutions, decentralization will revert to its appropriate status as a technical issue in the design of administrative institutions. We are not then in the midst of a portentous crisis of institutional authority. Indeed, if there is a crisis at all, it stems not from the long-term decline of participation but from its increase. Daniel Bell and Virginia Held have argued that a "community revolution," beginning slowly in the 1950s and picking up resources and ideology in the sixties, has so multiplied the number of veto groups in New York City that it has, paradoxically, created a sense of "powerlessness and consequent frustration." [17]

As in many issues of analytical conflict, it's possible to quibble about the merits of rival arguments while missing wholly their complementary insights. Classic democratic theory properly loaded the burden of popular participation in government upon electoral processes. The people's will is expressed in periodic moments of choice between two or more rival candidates for public office. In practice, a small but important range of issues having to do with local and state finances, has been subject to direct popular choice without the intervention of representatives. Early in the twentieth century, there was considerable enthusiasm in the United States for the extension of government by referendum. This enthusiasm has now considerably waned. The referendum allows individuals to express their preferences on only one issue at a time. People are permitted to say whether they want a particular school bond issue or fair housing law, but are not simultaneously forced to describe the ways in which they propose to cope with the implications of their choice. Legislative bargaining which accommodates diverse interests inhibits this irresponsible, bit-by-bit choice and encourages more complex and presumably wiser decision making.

At the same time as the referendum has failed to satisfy the demand for participation, the growth of government has reduced the value of general elections. The expansion in the range of government activities has multiplied the values which must be simultaneously considered by public officials and has shifted the burden of this consideration from legislatures and elected executives to administrative agencies. The devaluation of the legislator reduces the role of the man who elects him. Even, however, where legislatures and elected executives have retained the ability to define policy and to control its administration, the enlarged scope of activities has reduced the significance of electoral choice. A voter, after all, only requires enough information to discriminate between two or occasionally three or four candidates. The simplicity of this choice rewards voters for knowing only enough to make a very general estimate of the orientation of the candidate. Because this estimate is highly generalized, it is difficult to alter. Change in this estimate requires either a reorganization of values or a perception that a single issue totally outweighs all others. In the case of the American war in Indo-China, for example, electoral politics has only seemed promising when large portions of the electorate stopped believing that everyone wanted peace and started, I think properly, polarizing the alternatives.

There have been three types of response to the devaluation of electoral politics. The first, and closest to the politics of communications, is the call for improvement in the mass media. From the early nineteenth century demands that the press free itself from the partisan influences of party identification, to the current interest in equal-time and publicly-financed campaigning, the design of the mass media and the purported rationality of the citizen-elector have been intertwined. Without denigrating at all the significance of these issues, they hardly address the intrinsic limitations of the electoral process which does not ordinarily reward extensive knowledge. The gap between what is said on American television and what is known and understood is already so immense that additional saying oriented to electoral politics hardly looms as a major instrument to enlarge public understanding. The second response is to call for the return of functions to small governmental units. On the right, this is described as a return to local self-government, the keystone of democracy. On the left, it appears as proposals to reconstruct city processes so that neighborhoods may become self-governing. These calls to decentralization founder on two rocks. First the units remain connected. Indeed, some of the functions which are treated as most local, such as garbage collection, land use, and education, are deeply tied to very broad influences. Regrouping does not simplify the requirements for knowledge, even if it increases the likelihood of a particular political program.

The second rock is the intractable limit of electoral politics. At any scale, even the smallest, the legislators responsible for the general budgeting of resources must trade with one another, winning some battles, losing others, and developing a shared respect for the process of negotiation. They may try to mobilize public support to increase their influence in legislative bargaining or they may try to explain a problem in order to command popular assent. Basically, however, even at the smallest level, they want only to be generally trusted by the electorate so that they can legitimately enter the negotiating process. The more intimate their constituency or the more united by bonds of common identity, the smaller their need to reinforce this trust with detailed information. The electoral politics of small units ordinarily reduces the need for complex understanding.

The final response to the devaluation of electoral politics is to extend its expectations and practices into administrative agencies. This extension may take the form of the direct election of advisory boards or provisions for broad public hearings. At its most imaginative, however, it depends upon a realization that the citizen is not simply a client for a service, he is a part of the service system itself: parents educate their children, individuals buy and refurbish homes, workers change jobs and train themselves for new skills, patients administer more medicine than physicians.

As soon as this relationship is grasped, the rewards for both knowing and telling become apparent. A school system which wants to teach each child must broadly inform its parents. Not informing is presumptive evidence of not wanting. A planner who wants to influence land use must sophisticate his land users by sharing knowledge and values with them. A manpower training program must enter into the whole pattern in which jobs are selected, skills learned, and changes risked. Patients must understand the purposes and dynamics of medical care.

Hitching dreams of public understanding to the star of administrative politics will require a complex planning effort which extends into the internal operations of self-protective bureaucracies. It's impossible to imagine extended public understanding of agencies in which subordinates do not comprehend the process or substance of decision making, in which evaluative information is never gathered or is jealously guarded.

External pressure and the internal dynamics of many agencies combine to make this complex planning effort possible. It is an illusion, however, to imagine that this effort can be supported as a radical attack on political or social élites. The design of new communications systems will, rather, be generated by an establishment attack on barbarism. The richness of the design and its potential for counterinfluences will depend upon the level of imagination and commitment brought into the planning process by those who care enough not be distracted by illusions or immobilized by harsh realities.

The next chapter describes my image of the form these systems might take and the hazards in planning them.

SEVEN

COMMUNICATIONS POLICY:

Preparing the Table

When this book was first conceived, the books and articles I read were decisively down on the media. Driven by ambition and a costly technology, the lords of the press and airwaves were pictured as grouping larger and larger audiences together. The result of this aggregation was supposedly a withering away of diversity within the media and within the society they served. Newton Minow's characterization of television as a "wasteland" [1] resonated with the social critique of Eliot's poem: a world full of action but without meaning or purpose.

My first attempt to grapple with this intellectual perspective on the media assumed, perhaps in deliberate contrast, a decidedly positive tone. First, it appeared to me that each of the media had gone through a series of stages. In its early history, it was used by a few, usually wealthy, cognoscenti. As its technology was perfected, it diffused to large but undifferentiated audiences. In a final stage, each of the media and its audiences has, in turn, become increasingly differentiated. While large central city newspapers were in trouble, the suburban and small-city press was flourishing. Similarly, while the great general circulation magazines were moaning and a few were dying, new journals and revitalized giants with specialized editions promised more rather than less weekly and monthly print journalism.

The sequence was, of course, neither inexorable nor irreversible. The opening of a vast new international market for films during the 1950s, for example, had probably impeded or even temporarily reversed tendencies to differentiation in the movie industry. Even in films, however, the enrichment of audiences and the reduction of production costs promised a return to a pattern of specialization. It seemed to me in 1966 that the age of massive television would also come to an end and that it was particularly dangerous to build a social image around the temporary economics of a single medium.[2]

My second observation was that the groups which were disadvantaged by the existing pattern of differentiation were not the élite critics of the cultural wasteland but rather the poorest groups in American society. The call for better television was a form of special pleading by those whose cup was already largely full. Despite the universalistic claims of the proponents of high culture, I found it hard to believe (sharing the skepticism of Raymond Williams) [3] that they were particularly sensitive stewards of the cultural concerns of the poor.

As this book is actually written, I sense a change in the intellectual perspective on the media. The criticism of the fifties and early sixties has not died down. Instead it has been so amplified in a broad range of organizations [4] that it is now possible to move beyond moaning to action.

The most important basis for the new optimism is the enormous promise of new communication technologies. The cable connection of home television sets to broadcasting studios creates the possibility of offering twelve or twenty-four or even a hundred program channels to everyone. Sets may also be adapted to play recorded programs, transcribed off the cable or obtained from dealers. A combination of simple recording and facsimile transmission will make it possible to distribute newspapers and other printed materials directly to home information centers. Satellites, working in combination with local carrier systems, will radically extend the range of international communications. Computers and networks of computers have revived an eighteenth-century dream of universal encyclopedias offering every man equal access into vast shared memories.[5]

The technological promise has reinvigorated the sense of political possibility. The airways by acknowledged right are public property even more clearly than the land itself. Regulatory control of the cableways is firmly established. Though anyone would be naive to discount the enormous influence of established institutions such as television networks, their very salience and independent power makes them more amenable to rapid change than the great welter of local governments and agencies which dominate virtually every other functional system.

The possibility of new communications policies is reinforced by a constitutional connection. The prohibition against the passage of laws abridging the freedom of speech, or of the press need only be subtly transformed to present a mandate for action. The First Amendment may be read as an attack on all publicly endorsed or legitimated barriers to free speech and a prescriptive call to create the conditions under which discourse will flourish.[6] There is no similarly pointed constitutional mandate to ensure access to any other resource save perhaps due process and the right to vote.

In the midst of the current promise and optimism, it may seem ungracious of me—or simply perverse—to turn a skeptical cheek. The face is, I hope, nevertheless the same. In the midst of the pervasive complaint against massiveness, it was appropriate to emphasize the driving force of differentiation and expanded capacity. Now, with everyone alive to this drive, it seems equally appropriate to point out the implications of the various forms this differentiation and expansion may take.

Virtually all current writing on communications policy shares a common set of assumptions about the likely path of development. These assumptions unite the Federal Communications Commission and its critics. They are clearly expressed, for example, in a report by a prestigious commission gathered by the Sloan Foundation to recommend new policies for cable television.[7] The Sloan Commission, correctly anticipating restrictive FCC rules, urged in their place an expansive policy to encourage the growth of cable systems in large American cities. The commission, however, like the FCC itself, assumed that cable systems—

- would be privately initiated, or, if built by community development corporations, would be adapted to an essentially private national pattern.
- would be largely financed by subscriber fees.
- are an innovation in the delivery of television programming and, therefore, must be principally designed with an eye to their influence on the current stations and networks.
- are essentially bundles of channels.

All of the issues the Sloan Commission discussed, or that had been previously subject to intensive economic investigation by researchers at the RAND Corporation,[8] fit within these assumptions. These issues, including the allocation and control of channels and the financing of programming, are by no means trivial. They suffer, however, from the limitations of the framing assumptions. Proposals for change within this framework must necessarily be confined to the margins of established video practice.

There is another starting point for the design of new communications systems which is located within a framework of alternative assumptions. The skeleton of the alternatives is sketched in the following table:

ISSUE	ASSUMPTIONS CONVENTIONAL	ASSUMPTIONS PROPOSED
initiative	private	public
financing	subscribers	general treasury
innovative framework	established television	functional agencies and uses
scale of planning concern	channels	whole communications systems

The first two proposed assumptions are obvious. If a cable is a highway, may it not be built under highway-like auspices? They are also likely to be the most controversial, since they raise the combined spectres of socialism and thought control. The volume of controversy and the importance of the assumptions are, however, inversely related. In fact, the two final assumptions are the most important. Public initiative and financing is not a sufficient condition for the creation of new communications systems designed for public understanding. Publicly initiated systems which were controlled by the final two conventional assumptions would not fulfill their promise: mixed public and private enterprises operating with the two proposed alternatives might.

The weight of my argument rests on these two final assumptions. The bane of communications policy seems to me to be its name. A policy for communications directs attention to the industries which are designated as media and to the regulatory agencies which influence them. Suppose, however, we assumed instead that the transmission of information over cables—or, for that matter, from satellites—was an innovation in the design of schools, health clinics, police forces, business firms, and a host of other agencies whose day-to-day outpouring of messages dwarfs the flow of radio and television combined. This assumption would relegate most issues which now circumscribe cable growth to minor decisions to be settled near the end of a planning process.

Starting with functional systems would highlight the major limitation of the conventional framework. Where a cable or satellite is conceived as a bundle of channels, political decisions are narrowed to the allocation of these channels to groups and localities and to specifying the regulations which should govern their use. Even in imaginative proposals for public initiatives and connections between institutions, this narrow focus remains. An excellent MITRE Corporation study of Washington, D.C., for example, begins with the objective of meeting urban needs by wiring the city. The researchers then focus their attention on the overwhelming question, How much will the wires cost? [9]

If new communications systems are to serve established functions, the narrow focus must be expanded. There is more to a network than a channel. Adequate design and economic projections must be based upon a vision of channels, codes, and what I previously called intelligence centers, working together. Without such a vision, new systems will founder on the rocks of the old. Enhanced channel capacities do not necessarily increase the capacity of whole networks. Across the country, television sets in living rooms spew information without adding to knowledge, rest in classrooms without changing instructional practices.

There is a good deal that is both complex and difficult in starting with these proposed alternative assumptions. The established framework of media discussion cannot simply be set aside and forgotten. The new assumptions do not, however, suffer from that paradoxical ease and difficulty which attaches to remote suggestions which are not connected to any established organization. I do not propose that we begin with either a nonsystem, a countersystem, or a remote dream of the future city. I do not propose that we attack vested interests, only that we talk with different interests. Instead of convincing cable operators or network presidents we should focus on educators and police chiefs, physicians and community organizers, politicians and program analysts. Instead of wiping away all financial questions with vague allusions to the public treasury, we should enter communications expenditures, with all the required alliances, in the lists of claimants together with school buildings, health clinics, roads, squad cars, and community centers. Instead of presuming that television policy deals with a home-studio system, dependent on private initiatives and distinct from other information modes, we should be prepared to discuss publicly designed systems, linking diverse channels and functions in richly imagined, complex networks.

The initial difficulty of the alternative assumptions is that there is no established place and process for the new conversations. Where shall the table be to which police chiefs, schoolmen, and physicians can come? Who shall call the meeting? Who shall guide the discussions?

Only the unsatisfactory answers to these questions are readily apparent. The FCC cannot set the table; nor can television stations or private entrepreneurs. My guess is that conversations may begin within institutions and groups and then be carried forward cooperatively under the aegis of city or regional governments. These conversations around local tables will specify some tasks which can only be accomplished at the national level. The Congress and FCC may then substitute these specifications for the flabby criteria which currently guide their decisions. Until designers have met around local tables, no one in Washington knows how many channels are enough for education or health.

Local planning efforts are also likely to suggest experimental programs for subdivisions of the urban region. Indeed, it would be foolish to imagine any major policy initiatives without the guidance of experimental efforts. Communications technologies are peculiarly amenable to such experiments. It would be possible, for example, to build a new high capacity communications network in Harlem, North Philadelphia, or Scarsdale and then to decide after a few years that the network was a mistake and should be scratched. The same option is not, realistically, open to transportation planners who have to cope with awesome capital outlays. Where costs are high, as for example in highway construction, there are very few alternatives to cautious incrementalism. Communications systems are cheap enough for comprehensive planning.[10]

Someone, such as myself, sitting in an office removed from both the burdens and delights of power and responsibility cannot plan anything. The gravest danger of futurist thinking is the confusion of a compelling dream which establishes a theme for planning with a plan itself. The independent and irresponsible futurist is appropriately limited to spinning dreams, sketching their elements and the path of development, and to warning responsible men about the apprehensions their efforts will arouse as they move towards actual plan making.

Dreaming and warning are related functions. Generalized dreams require few cautions. The dream of expanded public understanding in the first chapter arouses few suspicions. As the dream becomes more specific—as it details a future educational or health delivery system—the apprehensions grow and planners require more guides to challenged values and imagined threats. The actual planning of any new system will be a complex process, requiring a cycling of concerns and specifications through levels of government and hierarchies of private institutions and organizations. The first threat—and the first task—will appear before this process can even fairly begin. The communications planner must develop and convey to all interested parties a sense of the whole process. If everyone suspects that the first decisions will determine the entire pattern of a system, then everyone will want to be admitted to the first stage. Paradoxically, extending the range of early claimants will narrow the imaginative scope of the planning process. Publishers and station owners, the Black Panthers and the League of Women Voters, the Welfare Rights Organization and the National Citizens Committee for Broadcasting, meeting together with educators, physicians, and librarians will find agreement simplest if they rely on the conventional assumptions. If the media on the one side and the organizations interested in occasional programming on the other are excluded from the first discussions, then new and more complex ideas may be explored.

If the first discussions can be confined to the representatives of large functional communications networks, the planner can pose and actively help answer a series of difficult questions:

> What are the capacities of your current communications networks?
>
> How do they condition the scope and effectiveness of your operations?
>
> Would new storage, retrieval, processing, and transmission capacities, at various levels, alter the scope, effectiveness, and location of your operations?
>
> What is the relationship between scope, effectiveness, and the way you organize and locate your physical facilities?

Each of the representatives will answer these questions in his own way. Some, despite the biased prodding of the communications planner, may insist that neither increased information management nor communications capacity would significantly alter his behavior. The general result is likely to be, however, a discovery that new communications capacity will increase the effectiveness and scope of their operations.

No one now can accurately predict the shape of the preferred network which will emerge from these discussions. The questions as posed should, however, avoid the limitations of the conventional focus on cable and video. That focus concentrates the tasks of internal and external integration, as described in the second chapter, upon the home information center. The viewer at home must connect what he sees with what he reads, must hear and be reminded, must understand and imagine action in isolation, with only the assistance of what is carried to him and projected on a screen.

I strongly suspect that this is an impossible connective task. As with current television broadcasting, many of the links will be outside the home so that the dream of separate castles of knowledge will be illusory. Educators and physicians, without the bias of the conventional focus, are likely to prepare designs which rest principally on small information centers scattered in every neighborhood, each with access to libraries, computers, video tape banks, mimeograph machines, and tape recorders. The centers would be staffed by guides to both information and action. Some would be multipurpose and would be designated, perhaps, as information centers. Others would serve specialized functions and would be miniversions of familiar institutions: small schools, little clinics, store-front police stations, neighborhood law offices, branches of the community college, or training centers for graduate engineers.

With the specifications for these facilities, and the networks supporting them, the communications planner can undertake the delicate task of creating a design which merges and compromises in order to enjoy the benefits of shared costs. The danger in this step may well be in the planner's preference for coordination. Many agencies will quite properly insist that they want their own computers and unique access into them. The insistence is not necessarily misplaced. There is an apparently inescapable balance between the complexity of a computational task and the number of effective terminals which a computer can support. Ask a repeated and simple question and the number is enormous. Ask a complex question, covering a range of issues with a great many back-and-forth interactions, and the number falls dramatically. The economics and practice of computation, rather than bureaucratic provincialism, may dictate to each his own.[11]

Apart from the scattered facilities and network, each of the agencies should have suggested channel requirements for video programming directly into homes. The planner's task, as I imagine it, is both to add these requirements so as to arrive at an estimated total and to complement them with three specifications which may not appear in the agency lists:

electronic feedback
accessible production facilities
accessible memories

Present electronic and print media only allow very indirect response from consumer to producer. You may turn to another channel when you don't like a program and find your displeasure captured by a random audience survey. You may write a letter to the editor or buy a product "in appreciation." Whatever purposes they serve, these feedback processes clearly do not increase the capacities for complexity in the medium itself. They do not, for example, allow television commentators to attempt more difficult explanations of contemporary affairs.

Increasing the number of channels is only a partial substitute for feedback. If you can say a great many different things, at different paces, in different codes, you are more likely to be responsive to individuals than if you are constrained to address mass audiences. The variety of individual postures is, however, much larger than any conceivable programming range. Moreover, people do not really know what they think until they have had a chance to talk. Only when they hear themselves can they compare ideas with each other and weigh their merits.

There are several different types of feedback mechanisms which are possible. A few experimental programs have used Touch-Tone telephones or ten-button audience voting mechanisms. A group of engineering students at the Moore School of the University of Pennsylvania, working on a communications system for North Philadelphia, developed a simple three-button system elaborated to measure the response of ninety thousand viewers roughly every two minutes.[12] I am not concerned here with the merits of any particular hardware but with a more general emphasis:

124

Any cable system built today should include a two-way capacity. Feedback is more important than channel numbers.

Feedback to the production center expressing an opinion, a measure of consent or understanding, or even a guess, when it is conveyed across the system becomes a produced message. Imagine, for example, that a land use planner is talking with residents of an area of single family homes who are considering a proposal to build a new apartment house in their neighborhood. He describes seven assumptions about the effects of the new facility upon them. "Which of the assumptions," he might ask, "is most important in your image of the future?" When the response comes back—a three-button system can discriminate seven alternatives—the planner would have a measure of attitudes and neighbors would know each other. They might, indeed, know each other better after a series of back and forths through the video intermediary than in the setting of backyards and community meetings with their strong pressure towards convergent thinking.

One of the seven items in the planner's display might be "None of the Above" or "Call me, you're missing the point." Nevertheless, even with these controls, the planner's position at the node of the communications system, shaping the questions and the transmission of responses, gives him very substantial influence over the flow of information. To prevent this influence from corrupting his authority, he must allow the consumers to become producers. Each one of the functional systems utilizing the network will have to allow individuals and groups access to the system. Experience in Montreal has demonstrated that this can be done both effectively and cheaply. Labor costs for live programming vary from about fifteen to a hundred dollars per hour. N. E. Feldman puts the case sharply:

> The minimum costs for local origination on noncommercial TV broadcast stations in the United States are about $3000 for one hour. Our estimate suggests that Canadian cable operators can generate ten to thirty hours per week of new local live programming at an hourly cost of no more than 2 to 4 percent of this figure. To be sure, the final product is not the same, but the ratio is impressive nevertheless.[13]

The final element which must be added to the agency specifications is access into enhanced memories or libraries. The prime body of information which must integrate with the channel capacities of the network is the record of the agency's performance: the school districts' evaluation reports and internal histories, the planning commission's record of land use change, the health system's input-output tables, the welfare department's program lists and records.

Linked to these discrete bodies of information, is a much larger memory associated with the conventional library. Libraries play a critical role in the integration of communication networks and the expansion of public competence. Broadening the class basis of their use has, however, proved extremely difficult. From early twentieth century experiments in readability to the latest extensions in book-mobiles and ethnic displays, small groups of professionals have struggled with this bias and attempted to reach out. They've been forced, however, to be thankful for very minor victories.[14]

The external integration of new electronic networks and the response and production capacities of its intelligence centers and channels may subtly alter library usage. Stored video tapes may prove an effective conduit into the world of print. It's very likely, however, that the general public library requires changes comparable to those developed and projected in large scholarly collections. We ordinarily conceive the items in a library, at one extreme, as books. The word *data bank*, at the other extreme, conjures an image of tiny notes, perhaps of sentence or numeral length. Most users require neither extreme most of the time. The appropriate unit of the first statement we ordinarily need is closer to a page. Given a question, explore a page, or small sets of pages. Satisfied with one you can stop the inquiry or move on along a chain of others.[15]

The ability to interact with his library in this form is essential for the research scientist. He winds his way through indices, abstracts, summaries, and review articles before he encounters the dense mass of books and articles themselves. The ordinary user has, however, no such convenient guides. As a result, books—popular, well-written and well-chosen as they may be—loom for many as a virtually impenetrable jungle.

Creating libraries which conquer this jungle is probably the hardest problem in the design of new communications networks.

Aggregating agency and group requirements and adding the complementary capacities is only the beginning of the planning process. In successive rounds, plans have to be broadened by a political and cultural vision which goes beyond both localism and agency-by-agency accounting. There are a great many groups in any city which will want to be heard and seen and whose message will not fit into neat categories: Black Panthers and garden clubs, young film and video tape makers,[16] temperance advocates, doves and hawks. Some will want to cover the city; others only small sections. Some will be able to pay their own way; others will require a subsidy for effective access. Some will need technical assistance; others will bring prepared tapes.

Describing the technological and organizational requirements of a system capable of carrying these messages is a demanding task. When I first imagined a new system, I expected that this task would be performed by a citizens group such as the Area Wide Council of the Philadelphia Model Cities program or the Bedford-Stuyvesant Corporation.[17] The intense political concerns of these groups now seem to me to impose obstacles to communicative openness and to impose unnecessary burdens on them. I would prefer to multiply the points of entry into the system and allow flexible networking of scattered areas. The apportionment of channel time, use of the response system, and production subsidies should be administered by accountable city-wide or regional agencies on the basis of publicly defined guidelines. Community development corporations would be freed to act as large-scale message producers rather than controllers.

The wide variety of groups which want to produce for television should also be encouraged to use the other media and to store their work in libraries. The production centers of the functional agencies or more generalized studios should be equipped, therefore, with typewriters and mimeograph and photo-offset printers. Libraries should be prepared to store what may seem at first ephemeral material from the streets. The first libraries of pages (rather than books) may be composed of broadsides produced by citizen action groups.

There is no confident way of predicting the impact of a municipal system of the sort I have described upon the established media. My guess is, however, that they would manage to adapt themselves with great skill and sustained profit. The efflorescence of local television talk is not likely to challenge the major role of the established networks and stations in providing dramatic and musical entertainment, sports, national and international news, and documentaries. The usual substance of programming may be subtly shifted as the networks and stations use feedback systems, and develop more discursive and sequential scheduling. Broadcasters are quite right, however, to discount the possibility that amateur hours and Little League Baseball would replace national professional stars.[18]

Similarly, the role of newspapers is likely to be enhanced by a communicative explosion which increases literacy. The newspapers have challenged the FCC effort to separate media ownerships. The premise of this FCC effort has been the desire to preserve media independence and diversity. With a vast range of channels and an obscured media boundary, reconsideration may be in order. Despite the current interest in aural and visual codes, the printed word preserves its powerful status as the most powerful mode of sequential, complex, and retrievable public communications. (It is precisely because it is so peculiarly powerful that it is so difficult to learn.) Ideally, audiences should be encouraged to move back and forth between one mode and another, exploiting the strengths of each. If newspapers can be encouraged to form a bridge for this movement, perhaps they should be allowed to buy into the electronic media.[19]

If the established media are not likely to be hurt by public initiatives, and may even profit from them, then, in the next round, planners should turn to the possibilities of public-private cooperation. A private CATV developer may still see rewards in the introduction of remote stations and the provision of specialized services despite—or because of—municipal efforts. With a firm sense of public requirements, a communications planner can enter into negotiations on shared costs and leased lines. Without this sense, he enters into discussions (as in city after city today) with penny ante requests for a channel here or there or a few more dollars in franchise taxes.

Cost sharing conversations should go beyond the realm of CATV developers. Private computer facilities, data communications firms (including Bell), processing services, and comprehensive computer utilities may all be interested in riding piggyback on a municipal system, or having public users as customers. The danger in these discussions is the trap of hidden subsidies. A city, or an aggressive suburban business center, might, for example, try to develop unique advantages for business firms by the provision of low-cost computer time sharing and internal telecommunication lines, as a counterpart to the accepted amenities of transportation and street movement. Subsidies of this sort are, however, likely to initiate a wave of comparable investments everywhere. The public would be left with a bill for a futile gesture. Cost savings should be shared; subsidies avoided.

I have described a very complex planning process. It violates the ordinary assumption that a free communications system will be privately initiated, but does not fit the mold of state ownership as we know it in Great Britain or Germany.[20] It mixes value and technical considerations rather than clearly isolating them. It demands an enormous amount of new thinking, bureaucratic coordination, and political patience. It challenges concepts such as "community control," "local issues," and "neighborhood," while serving some of their gods.

The general difficulties of a complex public process will be compounded in each of the functional systems. If information were unimportant, it would be easy to alter its flow. Because, however, a new distribution of knowledge alters relationships, it necessarily threatens satisfied interests and arouses fear. In the next few pages I have illustrated three of these fears, locating each in a particular institution. There is hardly an institution, however, which could enter into the planning of new communications systems without arousing within it most of the apprehensions I've sketched—and then some which cannot be anticipated.

FEAR	INSTITUTION
revision of institutional boundaries	universities
loss of independence	health care
displacement of priorities	criminal justice

It is not difficult to imagine a network of computers, libraries, cables, and micro-instructional centers serving higher education. From the outset of television broadcasting in this country, universities have perceived in the medium an enormous extension of their educational capacities. They have not been able to realize the promise of this extension, however, because of the limited number of available channels and the difficulty of recovering the costs of programming from eligible users. The creation of new high capacity networks would simultaneously alleviate both these problems.

This potential alleviation and the chances it offers for diffusing higher education may seem a glorious opportunity rather than a threat. From the outside it may appear so. From the perspective of an insider, however, the dangers may easily outweigh the glories. Institutions of higher education range from the most prestigious universities to entrepreneurial training schools. Each adapts to its local situation—the students it attracts, the faculty it assembles and organizes, the resources it can bring to bear upon its selected tasks—while at the same time preserving connections with the other institutions. The major connection is a shared body of knowledge, represented by libraries of books and journals. Since World War II, the paperback book and a flood of texts and so-called readers have increased the accessibility of this body of knowledge to every student. This increase is, in effect, an expanded interinstitutional linkage. The linkage revises the local role of the professor. Once he was a uniquely important link, conveying orally to his students what was being said, thought, and written in the centers of learning. Now it seems foolish to say what can be more efficiently read.

Professors, and the institutions in which they work, have been remarkably resistant to modifying their behavior to utilize this expanded connection. In hundreds of colleges and universities, bookstores and libraries have not been conceived as essential parts of the instructional process. Professors often assign a hundred pages of reading and then bring students together in class to say orally the equivalent of another ten or fifteen pages. These oral moments are the walls which protect the professor and the institution from the outside and preserve their local advantages as purveyors of knowledge.

A new technology and the pressure of rising costs now threatens these oral moments. It is possible—and I believe wise—for most lectures to be transcribed onto video tape, to be watched at a student's convenience, and, where he desires, over and over again.[21] Like books themselves, these tapes may be shared between institutions and viewed in homes or libraries scattered across the face of the country. A wired city or an interinstitutional network in a dense region such as the Northeast Corridor would make tape libraries particularly accessible.

The promise—or threat—of video tape is, ironically, much less than that of books. Like the final straw on the camel's back, however, it may break the grip of an established instructional process. Tapes can be combined with readings, interactive computer programs, and diagnostic tests to form teaching modules in place of courses. While the preparation and revision of these modules will take a great deal of effort and will encourage the growth of a hierarchy of supporting instructional workers and institutions, the gross effect of the change will be to free a great deal of professorial time for personal instruction and intense interaction with groups of students. The reduction of institutional isolation in this way paradoxically increases the possibilities of local adaptation. A teacher who must interact with students cannot afford for long simply to display his learning. He must listen, guide, and change, responsive to the flow of student activity and understanding.

The most obvious influences of new instructional technologies will be the extension of present experiments in universities of the air, or universities without campuses. Mature students with families or in mid-career will be able to study without major interruptions in their life patterns. The more striking—and threatening—influence, however, is likely to be felt within the walls of existing institutions. As the universities' instructional processes become more open and available, the nature of its student body and its demands should also subtly shift. As long as instruction requires being on-campus, it is efficient to concentrate the educational process upon those who have not yet begun their careers and families. The culture of most colleges and universities is built around the age segregation of the youth ghetto. If more students may study off-campus, and if campus experiences can then be shorter and more academically purposeful, the rationale for the age bias should be reduced. An open university is likely to be more demographically balanced than a closed one. Its culture will have to reflect the change.

This cultural change will come both in little rituals and social organizations and in the core of intellectual activities. Institutions of higher education are closely connected to the world of professional and skilled work. As you move down the hierarchy of educational institutions, the connection between educators and practitioners tends to become closer. At the top of the hierarchy, the roles are sharply separated and academic norms are more fully established as independent rules of behavior. When the connections are made between the two worlds, the marks of separate territory are preserved. A business executive coming to the university for a seminar is on the professor's turf. The professor acting as consultant is on the executive's territory and should not consider his advice as an act of public research or science.

Television systems already implemented in a few places breach this territorial boundary. University classes are transmitted directly into work sites to users who can pay the costs of the extension. Increased channel capacities in cable and satellite systems promise to reduce this cost and increase the range of this professional interpenetration. Mature students with experience at work will increasingly bring a sophisticated personal sense of the relevance of knowledge into their periods of campus learning.

These extensions of present influences will challenge the separateness of university norms; particularly the conception of disciplines as organizing units of knowledge and rewards. Some within the university, or within society at large, may see these challenges as salutary. (It is certainly not fashionable these days to defend the idea of disciplines.) Others, however, may be filled with foreboding. The differences in these perceptions already organize university debates on the largest purposes of education and the strategies for achieving them.

A municipal planner who convened officials from institutions of higher education to talk about a local or regional communications policy should be aware of all of these challenges and threats. If he recruits to his table the enthusiastic proponent of audio-visual and continuing education, he will start with a friend who understands his language but may be—indeed is likely to be—a weak reed upon which to lean. The task of the planner is both to initiate and cultivate a broadly based discussion within each institution on the nature of education as a communications process, rather than on the new technological additions to established practices. Building on this discussion, with representatives close to the levers of power in their institutions, he can move to experimental proposals whose success can be generalized rather than simply displayed as an expensive "modern," frill.

There is hardly a functional system operating in the city in which someone or another is not urging new investments in communications and information systems. There is similarly, hardly a system in which such investments do not arouse fears of loss of independence, over-centralization, and massive and rigid bureaucracies.

The information scientists and communication advocates have undoubtedly sometimes encouraged these fears by an overweening pride. Before anyone had actually gone about the task of designing a multiple access, shared-time computer, for example, there was a great deal of speculative talk about comprehensive data banks and all-purpose centralized computational facilities. It's difficult for the much more modest but realistic images of specialized but linked systems to catch up and preempt the grand dream.

Beyond overweening pride, some of the counterfears aroused by the new technology are based on conventions of language. In ordinary usage, centralization and diversity conjure up polar images. It is difficult to grasp the idea that diverse practices may simply be adaptations to local circumstances under a given set of constraints. If the constraints are changed, the capacity to adapt and experiment may be enhanced even if the range of overt behavior is reduced. The more likely circumstance, however, is that central investments will extend the range of diversity by opening options which were precluded by the scale and pattern of previous decision making. The provision of centralized information and the decentralization of initiatives are as likely to be linked possibilities as polar opposites.

Grasping this anomalous image is difficult in every system but particularly in those where the diverse units enjoy a substantial measure of independence and are not likely to be drawn into a planning process in which they can assess for themselves the distribution of benefits.

Health and medical care delivery systems seem to me to be the most outstanding examples of a genus plagued by the failure to grasp the anomalous image.

The plague begins, paradoxically, in the midst of almost universal agreement that sound health education is a prime claimant for channel time in a new communications system. Despite occasional jokes about turning the population into self-examining hypochondriacs, most physicians believe that people would benefit from more, and more professionally responsible, information about the care and treatment of their own bodies. Such an increase in health education requires, of course, an expansion of centralized investments to improve the performance of the most diverse and independent units in the whole system of medical care, the individual consumer and patient.

An expansion of health education, conceived in this way as individual self-knowledge, would make relatively modest demands upon channel capacities. The design of programming would, in addition, not be very controversial. Indeed, if substantial benefits can be obtained through increased public knowledge, the present networks seem perfectly capable of carrying the required messages.

Unfortunately, the individual conception of health education is rooted in a conception of disease and health which still has very powerful practical clout but very poor intellectual credentials. Disease is now understood by medical theorists, as a complex interaction between individuals and elements in their environment which may combine in a varied range of symptoms. The classic image of the search for disease (as if they were things rather than categories), agents of disease, and cures now appears to be a very partial approach to the analysis of syndromes of sickness. Good health requires a similarly enlarged conception and has to be distinguished from the simple absence of disease.[22]

The idea that knowledge of sickness, the appropriate attack on sickness, and the shaping of health requires a perspective on diverse elements of the environment expands the domain of an effective health education program, demands increased channel capacities, and spawns controversy. "War," we are told by a popular poster, "is not healthy for children and other living things." What about lead paint? malnutrition? loneliness? ignorance? intense stress? What about indifferent medical practice?

It is possible to cultivate systems to ask these questions, to explore the answers in particular environments, and to increase individual and collective capabilities of guiding behavior away from sickness and towards health. Even if there is a substantial range of institutional innovations, the systems cultivated are likely to be dominated by the present organizations whose mission is the delivery of medical services. The technology of both environmental and individual screening will be accommodated into a variant of the public health service and community hospital. A new emphasis on health creation will enlarge on fields now dominated by the idea of therapy. The enlargement, as in the current development of community mental health, may strain established procedures and roles but it will not abandon the institutional framework of the medical center. The center may be in a store front, it may have a citizen board with grass roots participation, but when the smoke of organizational battle clears, the tasks of information gathering, analysis, and diffusion will demand the highest levels of professional skill. Influence will flow to those who possess this skill.[23]

The political controversy which must surround the creation of a sophisticated health information and education service will reach into all the other elements of the medical delivery system. The veneer of universal agreement that education is a good thing will crack as the technology and organizations designed to diffuse information are applied to the practice of medicine itself. In health, as everywhere else, shifts in power will flow from a change in the distribution of knowledge. The paradox of the likely conflict, already emergent, is that the prime beneficiaries of new systems are likely to be their most outspoken critics.

Almost every proposal for reconfiguration of medical practice hinges upon an analysis of that practice as an information system. Populations are observed, symptoms compared against memories, and prescriptive action advised and monitored. Only in a few fields, such as surgery, does the physician command a unique manipulative skill separate from his ability as a perceptive observer and diagnostic memory.

The most general impact of new communications and information-processing technologies upon the practice of medicine is the equalization of access to information across physical and hence social spaces.

We now have—or could have, if we chose—the capability of providing to scattered general practitioners the diagnostic and prescriptive wisdom of specialists, either personally over television lines or in their extensions into computerized information systems. Heavily automated screening of large populations can also complement patient memories in a manner which can expand capabilities of treating very ordinary ailments such as headache and abdominal pain.

Pursuing this capability will be expensive. Access into computer-stored medical indices and libraries is still far from developed. Diagnostic computer programs are in their infancy. While the signal from any electronic measuring instrument can be transmitted over space, we have not yet organized any large population of physicians into diagnostic networks. The exciting experiment which links the infirmary at Logan Airport to Massachusetts General Hospital via closed circuit television is still an ungeneralized trial run.[24]

The men most immediately identified as proponents of reconfiguration, computers, and telecommunications are associated with large medical facilities. Most current investments in information systems are intended to rationalize the operations of such facilities. While, across the country, some private physicians have used computerized billing services, they by and large have not shared in the talk of new systems. They are instead treated as the enemy of systems planning, though they are, ironically, its most likely beneficiaries. Without substantially altering their work routines, the private individual or small group can enjoy professional advantages ordinarily available only at the center of current systems. In contrast, the men at the center will find their work routines substantially altered as their practice is refocused on research, the evaluation of performance, the up-dating of computer memories and analytic routines, and continuing professional education (substantially replacing the extensive educational force maintained by the drug and equipment manufacturers).

The municipal planner, as he invites people to work with him, may find in school districts and universities that his initial recruits are not centrally placed within their institutional hierarchies. He should be prepared to move up the line. In the field of health, he may wisely reverse the direction. The initial advocates of systems planning will be very influential in a few large institutions and in the national health agencies. He must bend over backwards to capture the attention of scattered practitioners and to engage them.

Proponents of a new technology or organization are always in danger of distorting problems in order to sell their own special solutions, listening with special patience and appreciation only to those who echo their distortion.

The system of criminal justice is, I believe, potentially the major site of a serious distortion of social priorities through the application of new communications technologies. The system is conventionally divided into four or (more honestly) five stages: monitoring the environment, apprehending likely criminals, judging them, punishing and/or rehabilitating those judged guilty. Across the country, police officials concerned with the first two stages have recognized the promise of new computer and remote communication capacities as extensions of their traditional interest in extended range and speed. To a lesser degree, innovative judicial administrators have understood that information systems are indispensable requirements of improved management. Planners will find police chiefs and administrators eager to talk about new communications systems. Their suspicions—if any—will be aroused only by fears that their own efforts will be diluted by new entrants and by requests for coordination.

Their eagerness is likely to be seductive. The Task Force on Science and Technology of the President's Commission on Law Enforcement (1967) honestly described the siren's call:

> Within the criminal justice system the greatest potential for immediate improvement by analysis and technological innovation appears to be in police operations. Hence police problems are emphasized heavily; less attention was given the problem of the courts; and still less to the inherently behavioral problems of corrections.[25]

Unfortunately, the seduction is a double illusion. Even if you assume that increased monitoring and apprehension reduces the incidence of crime, the new technology promises only small measures of amelioration. Remote sensing and visual inspection, as in television scanning of bank customers or department store shoppers, extends the policemen's ability to monitor the environment. In small settings, usually served by private control forces, this extended ability may inhibit or interrupt criminal activity. In the larger settings of streets and neighborhoods, homes and extensive public buildings, the deterrent effect, if any, hinges on the radical reduction of the time between a call for help and appearance of a policeman. Despite extensive technological investments in the reduction of response time, and even larger requests for further funds, policemen seem remarkably capable of adjusting their pace to avoid overrushing.[26]

The second illusion is more serious. Small measures of amelioration may be worth vast sums if there are no other competing options for improvement within the same problem area. Even if you put aside all consideration of reduction in the causes of crime, technological improvements in monitoring the environment and reducing the response time of policemen seem to me to be near the bottom—not the top—of the list of options. The top of the list, again ignoring the reduction of the causes of crime, includes decriminalization of some forms of deviant behavior, the creation of a rehabilitation system out of the ruins of punishment, and the expansion of the control capabilities and morale of local groups. Each of these activities may benefit from a general expansion of communications systems. None of them, however, is directly amenable to any significant measure of technological innovation and investment. New ideas, new organization, new facilities—but nothing very exciting on the frontiers of engineering or science.

It would be a bitter shame if we were seduced out of fighting crime by the claims of the crime fighters and a general belief in the mechanical symbols of innovation.[27]

The difficulties of the planning process I have sketched may seem awesome. Process descriptions are always more complex than policy mandates. They certainly lack the evocative clarity and neatness of prophesies of an inevitable future: inevitable because of a new generation, a new technology, or a new apocalypse.

In its favor, the process can start tomorrow. All it takes is the understanding by a great many men and women in scattered institutions, roles, and settings that communications policy is rich with implications for them, and the initiative of a relatively small number of government officials to begin preparing the table for discussion.

NOTES

ONE

1. Jay W. Forrester, *Urban Dynamics* (Cambridge: M.I.T. Press, 1969), p. 9.

2. Charles A. Reich, *The Greening of America* (New York: Random House, 1970).

3. For variations on this theme, sample the essays in *Toward the Year 2000: Work in Progress, Daedalus,* Summer, 1967; Donald N. Michael, *The Unprepared Society: Planning for a Precarious Future* (New York: Basic Books, 1968) and Alvin Toffler, *Future Shock* (New York: Random House, 1970).

4. Zbigniew Brzezinski argues this proposition vigorously in *Toward the Year 2000,* pp. 670–671. For a mixed appreciation see Daniel P. Moynihan, *Maximum Feasible Misunderstanding: Community Action in the War on Poverty* (New York: Free Press, 1969) and Raymond Aron, *Progress and Disillusion, The Dialectics of Modern Society* (New York: Frederick A. Praeger, 1968).

5. For sophisticated expressions of these views see Irving Kristol, "Urban Civilization and Its Discontents," *Commentary,* 50, no. 1 (July, 1970), pp. 29–35 and Roger Starr, "The Decline and Decline of New York," *New York Times Magazine,* November 21, 1971, p. 31.

6. Revised estimates of the increase in the Gross National Product strengthen this perspective. A. W. Sametz, "Production of Goods and Services: The Measurement of Economic Growth," in *Indicators of*

Social Change: Concepts and Measurements, eds. Eleanor Bernert Sheldon and Wilbert E. Moore (New York: Russell Sage Foundation, 1968), pp. 77–96.

7. Beverly Duncan and Stanley Lieberson, *Metropolis and Region in Transition* (Beverly Hills: Sage Publications, 1970) describes long-term patterns in the urban system.

8. The general psychological model used here, and throughout the book, is described in George A. Miller, Eugene Galanter and Karl H. Pribram, *Plans and the Structure of Behavior* (New York: Holt, Rinehart and Winston, 1960).

TWO

1. The influential work shaping my thinking was Richard L. Meier, *A Communications Theory of Urban Growth* (Cambridge: M.I.T. Press, 1962).

2. I've learned most of what I know in these matters from Kenneth Paul Fox's dissertation, "The Census Bureau and the Cities: National Development of Urban Government in the Industrial Age: 1870–1930," (typescript, University of Pennsylvania, 1972).

3. The example illustrates the points made, rather more abstractly, by Melvin Webber. See his essay, "The Urban Place and the Nonplace Urban Realm," in Melvin M. Webber, et al., *Explorations into Urban Structure* (Philadelphia: University of Pennsylvania Press, 1964), pp. 79–153.

4. The term is taken from Herbert J. Gans, *The Urban Villagers: Group and Class in the Life of Italian Americans* (Glencoe, Ill.: Free Press, 1962).

5. Claude E. Shannon and Warren Weaver, *The Mathematical Theory of Communication* (Urbana: University of Illinois Press, 1949); J. R. Pierce, *Symbols, Signals and Noise: The Nature and Process of Communication* (New York: Harper & Row, 1961) and Elwyn Edwards, *Information Transmission* (Condon, U.K.: Chapman and Hall, 1964) explicates the mathematical theory and its extensions.

6. George A. Miller, Eugene Galanter, and Karl H. Pribram, *Plans and the Structure of Behavior* (New York: Holt, Rinehart and Winston, 1960), pp. 125–138; Walter Reitman, "What Does It Take To Remember?" in *Models of Human Memory,* ed. Donald A. Norman (New York: Academic Press, 1970), pp. 469–509.

7. Dell Hymes, ed., *Language in Culture and Society: A Reader in*

Linguistics and Anthropology (New York: Harper & Row, 1964), pp. 215–220, 385–390.

8. John P. Robinson, Jerrold G. Rusk, and Kenra B. Head, *Measures of Political Attitudes* (Ann Arbor: Institute for Social Research, The University of Michigan, 1968), includes a section on the measurement of public information, pp. 411–422.

9. President's Task Force on Communications Policy, "Staff Paper I —A Survey of Telecommunications Technology," (Springfield, Va.: Clearinghouse for Federal Scientific and Technical Information, June, 1969), pp. 6–9.

10. I worked out the image of the shifting curve in conversations with Prof. Garth S. Jowett of the School of Journalism, Carleton University, Ottawa, Canada. Prof. Jowett's doctoral dissertation at the University of Pennsylvania (1972)—"Media Power and Social Control: The Motion Picture in America, 1894–1936"—analyzes the impact of the shift on the reception of films in the United States.

11. Robinson, Rusk and Head, *Measures of Political Attitudes*, p. 39.

12. Bradley S. Greenberg and Brenda Dervin, *Use of the Mass Media by the Urban Poor* (New York: Praeger, 1970), pp. 31–49.

13. See the special issue on "Illiteracy in America," *Harvard Educational Review*, 40, no. 2 (May, 1970).

14. Bernstein's work is carefully explicated, criticized and extended by Denis Lawton, *Social Class, Language and Education* (New York: Schocken Books, 1968).

15. Being lower class means, for Banfield, speaking restrictively and planning only over short time periods. Edward C. Banfield, *The Unheavenly City: The Nature and Future of Our Urban Crisis* (Boston: Little, Brown, 1970).

16. William Labov, "The Logic of Nonstandard English," in *Language and Poverty: Perspectives on a Theme,* ed. Frederick Williams (Chicago: Markham, 1970), p. 158.

THREE

1. Lewis Mumford, *The City in History: Its Origins, Its Transformations, and its Prospects* (New York: Harcourt, Brace & World, 1961).

2. The general framework of urban economic history and theory is sketched by Eric E. Lampard, "The Evolving System of Cities in the United States: Urbanization and Economic Development," in *Issues in Urban Economics,* eds. Harvey S. Perloff and Lowdon Wingo, Jr. (Balti-

more: Johns Hopkins Press, 1968), pp. 81–139. The application of existing theory to planning is described by Lloyd Rodwin, *Nations and Cities: A Comparison of Strategies for Urban Growth* (Boston: Houghton Mifflin, 1970). William Alonso emphasizes the difficulties of the analytical questions in "The Mirage of New Towns," *The Public Interest,* no. 19 (Spring, 1970), pp. 3–17.

3. Brian J. L. Berry, "Research Frontiers in Urban Geography," in *The Study of Urbanization,* eds. Philip M. Hauser and Leo F. Schnore (New York: John Wiley & Sons, 1965), p. 412. See also Berry's essay with Elaine Neils, "Location, size, and shape of cities as influenced by environmental factors: the urban environment writ large," in *The Quality of the Urban Environment: Essays on "New Resources" in an Urban Age* ed. Harvey S. Perloff (Baltimore: Johns Hopkins Press, 1969), pp. 257–302.

4. The major statement of purposes is a report by the Advisory Commission on Intergovernmental Relations, *Urban and Rural America: Policies for Future Growth* (Washington, D.C.: Government Printing Office, April, 1968). Many of the Commission's assumptions are embedded in the Urban Growth and New Development Act of 1970.

5. Ian L. McHarg, *Design With Nature* (Garden City, New York: Natural History Press, 1969).

6. This is virtually the only purpose which William Alonso, "The Mirage of New Towns," is disposed to accept. See also M. Lawrence Heideman, Jr., "Controlled Prospective Experiments in Planned Development of New Urban Units," *Archives of Environmental Health,* 18 (January, 1969), 72–95.

7. John T. Howard, "The Crisis of Cities: People in Space," in *A Nation of Cities: Essays on America's Urban Problems,* ed. Robert A. Goldwin (Chicago: Rand McNally, 1968), p. 82; James L. Sundquist, "Where Shall They Live?" *The Public Interest,* no. 18 (Winter, 1970), p. 90.

8. Garrett Hardin, "Everybody's Guilt: The Ecological Dilemma," *California Medicine,* 113 (November, 1970), p. 43.

9. R. Buckminister Fuller, *Comprehensive Thinking* (Carbondale, Illinois: Southern Illinois University, 1965); Marshall McLuhan, *Understanding Media: The Extensions of Man* (New York: McGraw-Hill, 1964).

10. Charles T. Meadow, *The Analysis of Information Systems: A Programmer's Introduction to Information* (New York: John Wiley & Sons, 1967); Manfred Kochen, ed., *The Growth of Knowledge, Readings on Organization and Retrieval of Information* (New York: John Wiley &

Sons, 1967); Committee on Information in the Behavioral Sciences, Division of Behavioral Sciences of the National Research Council, *Communication Systems and Resources in the Behavioral Sciences* (Washington, D.C.: National Academy of Sciences, 1967).

11. Albert Rees, "Information Networks in Labor Markets," *American Economic Review,* 56 (May, 1966), pp. 559–566.

12. Daniel J. Elazar, "Are We a Nation of Cities?" in *A Nation of Cities,* ed. Robert A. Goldwin, pp. 89–114; Pittsburgh Regional Planning Association, *Region With a Future,* Economic Study of the Pittsburgh Region, vol. 3 (Pittsburgh: University of Pittsburgh Press, 1963), pp. 39–40.

13. Committee on Telecommunications, National Academy of Engineering, *Communications Technology for Urban Improvement* (Washington, D.C.: National Academy of Engineering, June, 1971), pp. 174–175.

14. David Harrison, Jr. and John F. Kain, "An Historical Model of Urban Form," (Harvard University, Program on Regional and Urban Economics, Discussion Paper No 63, September, 1970), p. 11.

15. Gideon Sjoberg, *The Preindustrial City: Past and Present* (New York: Free Press, 1960); Leo F. Schnore, "On the Spatial Structure of Cities in the Two Americas," in *The Study of Urbanization,* eds. Hauser and Schnore, pp. 347–398.

16. Adna Ferrin Weber, *The Growth of Cities in the Nineteenth Century: A Study in Statistics* (Ithaca: Cornell University Press, 1963. Original edition, 1899), pp. 446–475.

17. Theodore R. Anderson and Janice A. Egeland, "Spatial Aspects of Social Area Analysis," *American Sociological Review,* 26 (1961), pp. 392–398; Brian J. L. Berry, "Cities as Systems Within Systems of Cities," in *Regional Development and Planning: A Reader,* eds. John Friedmann and William Alonso, (Cambridge: M.I.T. Press, 1964), pp. 125–129.

18. The suburban myth is reviewed and criticised by Bennett M. Berger, *Working-Class Suburb: A Study of Auto Workers in Suburbia* (Berkeley: University of California Press, second printing with a new preface, 1968).

19. E. Franklin Frazier, *Black Bourgeoisie* (Glencoe, Ill.: Free Press, 1957).

20. S. M. Miller, *et al.,* "Poverty, Inequality and Conflict," *The Annals of the American Academy of Political and Social Science,* 373 (September, 1967), pp. 16–52; Julius Margolis, "The Demand for Urban Public Services," in Perloff and Wingo, *Issues in Urban Economics,* pp. 527–565.

21. Anthony Downs, *Urban Problems and Prospects* (Chicago: Markham, 1970), pp. 6–74.

22. Jane Jacobs, *The Death and Life of Great American Cities* (New York: Random House, 1961).

23. Boris Pushkarev's "The Present Situation—Its Implications," Conference 2020, New York, January 30 and 31, 1969, pp. 33–34.

24. W. B. Bennett, "Cross-Section Studies of the Consumption of Automobiles in the United States," *American Economic Review,* 62 (1967), pp. 841–850.

25. The literature is reviewed by Suzanne Keller, *The Urban Neighborhood: A Sociological Perspective* (New York: Random House, 1968).

26. Richard Sennett, *The Uses of Disorder: Personal Identity and City Life* (New York: Alfred A. Knopf, 1970).

FOUR

1. The major statements of these positions are James S. Coleman *et al., Equality of Educational Opportunity* (Washington, D.C.: Government Printing Office, 1966) and United States Commission on Civil Rights, *Racial Isolation in the Public Schools* (Washington, D.C.: Government Printing Office, 1967).

2. James S. Coleman, "The Concept of Equality of Educational Opportunity," in Harvard Educational Review, *Equal Educational Opportunity* (Cambridge: Harvard University Press, 1969), pp. 9–24; Meyer Weinberg, *Race and Place: A Legal History of the Neighborhood School* (Washington, D.C.: Government Printing Office, 1967); "Serrano v. Priest: Implications for Educational Equality," *Harvard Educational Review,* 41, no. 4 (November, 1971), pp. 501–534.

3. The best extended history of this conflict is Lawrence A. Cremin, *The Transformation of the School: Progressivism in American Education* (New York: Alfred A. Knopf, 1961).

4. Stanley Lebergott, *Manpower in Economic Growth: The United States Record Since 1800* (New York: McGraw-Hill, 1964); Peter M. Blau and Otis Dudley Duncan, *The American Occupational Structure* (New York: John Wiley & Sons, 1967).

5. Beverly Duncan, "Trends in Output and Distribution of Schooling," in *Indicators of Social Change: Concepts and Measurements,* eds. Eleanor Bernert Sheldon and Wilbert E. Moore (New York: Russell Sage Foundation, 1968), pp. 601–672.

6. Martin A. Trow, "The Second Transformation of American Secondary Education," *International Journal of Comparative Sociology,* 2 (1961), pp. 144–166.

7. There is an important discussion of the significance of these ideas

in the early stages of public school development in Michael B. Katz, *The Irony of Early School Reform: Educational Innovation in Mid-Nineteenth Century Massachusetts* (Cambridge: Harvard University Press, 1968), and *Class, Bureaucracy & Schools: The Illusion of Educational Change in America* (New York: Praeger, 1971).

8. F. L. Strodtbeck, "The Hidden Curriculum of the Middle Class Home," in *Education of the Disadvantaged*, eds. H. Passow, M. Goldberg and E. J. Tannenbaum (New York: Holt, Rinehart and Winston, 1967), pp. 244–259.

9. Walter Loban, *The Language of Elementary School Children* (Champaign, Ill.: National Council of Teachers of English, 1963); John H. Flavell, *The Development of Role-Taking and Communication Skills in Children* (New York: John Wiley, 1968).

10. Joshua A. Fishman, *et al., Language Loyalty in the United States* (The Hague: Mouton, 1966).

11. There is a striking stability in these positions. Compare with examples of recent practice the old studies by Charles E. Merriam, *Civic Education in the United States* (New York: Charles Scribners, 1934) and Bessie L. Pierce, *Civic Attitudes in American School Textbooks* (Chicago: University of Chicago Press, 1930).

12. See the discussion of the curriculum entitled "Man: A Course of Study," in Jerome Bruner, *Toward a Theory of Instruction* (Cambridge: Harvard University Press, 1966), and Richard M. Jones, *Fantasy and Feeling in Education* (New York: New York University Press, 1968).

13. The general framework of this approach to stratification is developed in Edward O. Laumann, *Prestige and Association in an Urban Community: An Analysis of an Urban Stratification System* (Indianapolis, Bobbs-Merrill, 1966). Its implications for schooling are detailed in James S. Coleman, *The Adolescent Society* (New York: Free Press, 1961).

14. Herbert J. Gans, "Negro Problems and White Fantasies," in his *People and Plans: Essays on Urban Problems and Solutions* (New York: Basic Books, 1968), pp. 317–320.

15. Richard J. Margolis, "The Two Nations at Wesleyan University," *The New York Times Magazine*, January 18, 1970, p. 9.

16. James B. Conant, *Slums and Suburbs: A Commentary on Schools in Metropolitan Areas* (New York: McGraw–Hill, 1961).

17. Phillip W. Jackson, *The Teacher and the Machine* (Pittsburgh: University of Pittsburgh Press, 1968) and *Life in Classrooms* (New York: Holt, Rinehart and Winston, 1968).

18. P. Lauter, "Short, Happy Life of the Adams-Morgan Community

School Project," *Harvard Education Review,* 38 (1968), pp. 235–262.

19. Deborah I. Offenbacher, "Cultures in Conflict: Home and School as Seen Through the Eyes of Lower-Class Students," *The Urban Review,* 2 (May, 1968), pp. 2–8; Elizabeth M. Eddy, *Walk the White Line: A Profile of Urban Education* (Garden City, New York: Anchor Books, 1967).

FIVE

1. The phrase is from the title of the so-called Bundy Report. Mayor's Advisory Panel on Decentralization of the New York City Schools, *Reconnection for Learning: A Community School System for New York City* (November 9, 1967).

2. Herbert J. Gans, "The Mass Media as an Educational Institution," *The Urban Review,* 2 (February, 1967), pp. 5–10.

3. R. Buckminster Fuller, *Education Automation: Freeing the Scholar to Return to His Studies* (Carbondale, Ill.: Southern Illinois University Press, 1964), p. 50.

4. Phillip W. Jackson, *The Teacher and the Machine* (Pittsburgh: University of Pittsburgh Press, 1968), particularly clarifies this issue. See also a symposium wrestling with the perceived conflict between televised instruction and inquiry learning. Wilma McBride, ed., *Inquiry: Implications for Televised Instruction* (Washington, D.C.: National Education Association, 1966).

5. Robert M. Gagné, "Learning and Communication," in *Educational Media: Theory and Practice,* eds. Raymond M. Wiman and Wesely C. Meierhenry (Columbus, Ohio: Merrill, 1969), pp. 93–114.

6. Herbert R. Kohl, *The Open Classroom: A Practical Guide to a New Way of Teaching* (New York: A New York Review Book distributed by Random House, 1969).

7. Kenneth Clark, "Alternative Public School Systems," in *Harvard Educational Review, Equal Educational Opportunity* (Cambridge: Harvard University Press, 1969); "Education Vouchers—Peril or Panacea?" *Teachers College Record,* 22 (1971), pp. 325–387; Martin T. Katzman, *The Political Economy of Urban Schools* (Cambridge: Harvard University Press, 1971).

8. Allan W. Wicker, "School Size and Student's Experiences in Extra Curricular Activities," *Educational Technology,* 9 (1969), pp. 214–247.

9. The growth of management capability has been curiously detached from ideas about substantive change in instructional systems. See, as

evidence of the detachment, Frank W. Banghart, *Educational Systems Analysis* (New York: Macmillan, 1969).

10. Neal Gross, Joseph B. Giaquinta and Marilyn Bernstein, *Implementing Organizational Innovations: A Sociological Investigation of Planned Educational Change* (New York: Basic Books, 1971).

11. The proposed system is similar to that already developed in the Portland, Oregon, public schools by Dr. Donald W. Stotler.

SIX

1. See, for examples of this perception, Jane Addams, *Twenty Years at Hull House* (New York: Macmillan, 1916) and Lillian D. Wald, *The House on Henry Street* (New York: Henry Holt, 1915).

2. I am particularly sensitive on this point since my own book on New York City has sometimes been misread as a plea for a return to bossism. *Boss Tweed's New York* (New York: John Wiley, 1965).

3. Roger Lane, *Policing the City: Boston 1822–1885* (Cambridge: Harvard University Press, 1967).

4. Compared to industrial firms, of course, police initiatives and decision making is enormously decentralized. James Q. Wilson, *Varieties of Police Behavior: The Management of Law and Order in Eight Communities* (Cambridge: Harvard University Press, 1968).

5. John S. Saloma, *Congress and the New Politics* (Boston: Little, Brown, 1969); Robert L. Chartrand, Kenneth Janda and Michael Hugo, eds., *Information Support, Program Budgeting and the Congress* (New York: Spartan Books, 1968); Kenneth L. Kraemer, "The Systems Approach in Urban Administration—Planning, Management and Operations," Council of Planning Librarians, Exchange Bibliography 49 (Monticello, Ill.: Council of Planning Librarians, May, 1968).

6. Rachel Greenberg, Taner Oc and John Mosely clarified this point for me in a study of the Southeast Philadelphia Neighborhood Health Center.

7. Malcolm S. Knowles, *The Adult Education Movement in the United States* (New York: Holt, Rinehart and Winston, 1962).

8. John W. C. Johnstone and Ramon J. Rivera, *Volunteers for Learning: A Study of the Educational Pursuits of American Adults* (Chicago: Aldine, 1965).

9. The best known statement of this position is Milton Kotler, *Neighborhood Government: The Local Foundations of Political Life* (Indianapolis: Bobbs-Merrill, 1969). The array of positions is sympathetically

reviewed by Alan A. Altshuler, *Community Control: The Black Demand for Participation in Large American Cities* (New York: Western Publishing Company, 1970).

10. Allen F. Davis, *Spearheads for Reform: The Social Settlements and The Progressive Movement* (New York: Oxford University Press, 1967); Frances Fox Piven and Richard A. Cloward, *Regulating the Poor: The Functions of Public Welfare* (New York: Pantheon, 1971).

11. Roy Lubove, *The Professional Altruist: The Emergence of Social Work As a Career, 1880–1930* (Cambridge: Harvard University Press, 1965).

12. Monna Heath and Arthur Dunham, *Trends in Community Organization, A Study of the Papers on Community Organization Published by the National Conference on Social Welfare, 1874–1960* (Chicago: School of Social Service Administration, University of Chicago, 1963), is a guide to professional images and activities.

13. *Community Organization, 1958. Papers Presented at the 85th Annual Forum of the National Conference on Social Welfare* (New York: Columbia University Press, 1958).

14. Davis, *Spearheads for Reform,* pp. 148–217.

15. National Federation of Settlements and Neighborhood Centers, *Making Democracy Work: A Study of Neighborhood Organization* (New York, 1968).

16. "Today," Governor Nelson Rockefeller recently argued, "New York City has neither an effective citywide, old-line political organization with all its faults but eager to respond to the individual's needs, nor does it have true community or neighborhood elective government with the power to be either responsive to the people or accountable to them in meeting their needs." *New York Times,* 19 January 1972, p. 20.

17. Daniel Bell and Virginia Held, "The Community Revolution," *The Public Interest,* no. 16 (Summer, 1969), pp. 142–177.

SEVEN

1. Minow was Chairman of the Federal Communications Commission when he used the term in an address before the National Association of Broadcasters in May, 1961. Newton N. Minow, *Equal Time: The Private Broadcaster and The Public Interest,* edited by Lawrence Laurent (New York: Atheneum, 1964), pp. 48–64.

2. A paper I wrote at the center for Advanced Study in the Behavioral Sciences in 1966 was subsequently delivered at the Annual Meeting of

the American Political Science Association, September, 1967, and then revised under a new title, "Spatial and Temporal Perspectives in the United States City."

3. Raymond Williams, *Culture and Society, 1780–1950* (New York: Columbia University Press, 1958) and *Britain in the Sixties: Communications* (Baltimore: Penguin Books, 1962).

4. A convenient list is provided by Nicholas Johnson, *How to Talk Back To Your Television Set* (Boston: Little, Brown, 1970), pp. 211–214.

5. James Martin, *Future Developments in Telecommunications* (Englewood Cliffs, N.J.: Prentice-Hall, 1971); Harold Sackman, *Mass Information Utilities and Social Excellence* (Princeton: Auerbach, 1971).

6. Jerome A. Barron, "Access to the Press—A New First Amendment Right" *Harvard Law Review* 80 (1967): 1641–1678.

7. Sloan Commission on Cable Communications, *On The Cable: The Television of Abundance* (New York: McGraw-Hill, 1971).

8. Leland L. Johnson, *The Future of Cable Television: Some Problems of Federal Regulation* (January, 1970) and *Cable Television and the Question of Protecting Local Broadcasting* (October, 1970); Richard A. Posner, *Cable Television: The Problem of Local Monopoly* (May, 1970); N. E. Feldman, *Cable Television: Opportunities and Problems in Local Program Origination* (September, 1970); Rolla Edward Park, *Potential Impact of Cable Growth on Television Broadcasting* (October, 1970) and *Cable Television and UHF Broadcasting* (January, 1971).

9. *Urban Cable Systems* (Washington, D.C.: MITRE Corporation, November, 1971).

10. My position is similar to that expounded in David Braybrooke and Charles E. Lindblom, *A Strategy of Decision: Policy Evaluation as a Social Process* (New York: Free Press, 1963). Incrementalism does not preclude comprehensive design where the risks and costs are relatively small. Indeed, where bit-by-bit clearly promises failure, there is little reasonable alternative to comprehensiveness.

11. Gene M. Amdahl, "Architecture for On-Line Systems," in *Computers and Communications—Toward a Computer Utility,* ed. Fred Gruenberger (Englewood Cliffs, N.J.: Prentice-Hall, 1968), pp. 109–117.

12. "COMNET: A Proposed Communication Network for North-Central Philadelphia," (mimeo, Moore School of Electrical Engineering, University of Pennsylvania, May 8, 1969).

13. N. E. Feldman, *Cable Television: Opportunities and Problems in Local Program Organization,* pp. 7–8.

14. I've benefited from talking about libraries with Harlan T. Crider

and Mrs. Leonard Feldman. The issues of class bias are broadly discussed in Ralph W. Conant, ed., *The Public Library and the City* (Cambridge: M.I.T. Press, 1965) and in a series of more specialized reports by individual libraries.

15. J. C. R. Licklider, *Libraries of the Future* (Cambridge: M.I.T. Press, 1965); Michael A. Duggan, Edward F. McCartan, and Manley R. Irwin, eds., *The Computer Utility: Implications for Higher Education,* (Lexington, Mass.: D.C. Health, 1970).

16. The remarkable efflorescence of these groups can be followed in issues of the journal *Radical Software,* published in New York since 1970.

17. The germ of an idea was planted in Bedford-Stuyvesant by Stephen White, "Toward a Modest Experiment in Cable Television," *The Public Interest,* no. 12 (Summer, 1968), pp. 52–66. The trials of the Area Wide Council are described in paired articles " 'Maximum Feasible Manipulation' in Philadelphia", and "Postscript: The Conflict in Context," *City,* 4 (October/November, 1970), pp. 30–43.

18. See the report of the reassuring memorandum from Julian Goodman, president of the National Broadcasting Company, to his staff, *New York Times,* 7 December 1970, p. 91.

19. The newspapers, it should be fairly noted, have not phrased their arguments in these terms. "Comments of the American Newspaper Publishers Association in Opposition," Federal Communications Commission, In the Matter of Amendment of Sections 73.5, 73.240 and 73.636 of the Commission's Rules Relating to Multiple Ownership of Standard, FM and Television Broadcast Stations, Docket No. 18110.

20. Wilson P. Dizard, *Television: A World View* (Syracuse: Syracuse University Press, 1966).

21. Robert Dubin and R. Alan Hedley, *The Medium May Be Related to the Message: College Instruction by TV* (Eugene: Center for the Advanced Study of Educational Administration, University of Oregon, 1969) comprehensively review evaluations of television instruction.

22. Alan Sheldon, "Toward a General Theory of Disease and Medical Care," in Alan Sheldon, Frank Baker, and Curtis P. McLaughlin, eds. *Systems and Medical Care* (Cambridge: M.I.T., 1970), pp. 84–125.

23. Warren Suss and Victor Crown have helped to clarify these issues for me.

24. Konrad K. Kalba, "Communicable Medicine: Cable Television and Health Services" (mimeo, Sloan Commission on Cable Communications, May, 1971). Michael Crichton, *Five Patients: The Hospital Explained*

(New York: Alfred A. Knopf, 1970) describes the Logan-Massachusetts General connection.

25. The Institute for Defense Analysis, *Task Force Report: Science and Technology*. A Report to The President's Commission on Law Enforcement and Administration of Justice (Washington, D.C.: Government Printing Office, 1967), p. 5.

26. The Organization for Social and Technical Innovation, *Implementation*. Submitted to the President's Commission on Law Enforcement and Administration of Justice (mimeo, 1967), pp. 42–43.

27. William Cozzens, Roseanne Levin, and Brenda Manning, have helped to develop this skeptical posture.

A native of New York City, Seymour Mandelbaum attended Columbia University and received his Ph.D. from Princeton in 1962. In 1965 he was awarded a Guggenheim fellowship. He now lives in Philadelphia and teaches at the University of Pennsylvania in the departments of History and City and Regional Planning. He is married and has three children.